THE
THERAPEUTIC
TRIANGLE

THE THERAPEUTIC TRIANGLE

A Sourcebook On Marital Therapy

CARLFRED B. BRODERICK

SAGE PUBLICATIONS
Beverly Hills / London / New Delhi

For information address:

SAGE Publications, Inc.
275 South Beverly Drive
Beverly Hills, California 90212

SAGE Publications India Pvt. Ltd.
C-236 Defence Colony
New Delhi 110 024, India

SAGE Publications Ltd
28 Banner Street
London EC1Y 8QE, England

Printed in the United States of America

Library of Congress Cataloging in Publication Data

Broderick, Carlfred B.
    The therapeutic triangle.

    Bibliography: p.
    1. Marital psychotherapy. I. Title. [DNLM:
1. Marital therapy. 2. Interpersonal relations.
3. Professional-patient relations. WM 55 B864t]
RC488.5.B69   1983   616.89'156   82-23062
ISBN 0-8039-1943-3

FIRST PRINTING

contents

Preface   7

**Part I: The Theory and Practice of
          Triangular Therapy   9**

1   A Basic Model for Triangular Therapy   11
2   The Fine Art of Establishing Triangular Rapport:
     The Principle of Symmetricality   23
3   The Fine Art of Establishing Triangular Support:
     The Principle of Therapist Potency   37
4   Diagnosing Couples' Problems   49
5   Establishing the Triangular Therapeutic
     Contract   67

Part II: Achieving Effective Change   91

6   Changing Behaviors   93
7   Changing Perspectives   115
8   Changing Feelings   137
9   Dissolving the Therapeutic Triangle   155
10   Physician, Heal Thyself   169
A Final Word   179
References   181
About the Author   183

preface

For over 25 years I have been doing couples' therapy, and for nearly half of that time I have been teaching doctoral students how to do it. Like most therapists of every type, I see a substantial number of individual clients in the traditional one-on-one format. And I both treat and supervise the treatment of whole families (or major segments of them), which involves the clinician with three or four or more people at a time. But what I love best and what I do best is triangular therapy.

There is something about the complexity of the marital bond, something about the skill required to maintain a balance against pressures to side with one or the other, something about the challenge of finding just the right blend of interventions that results in a couple's mastering their own problems—something about all of this that is beguiling and satisfying to me.

In this small book I have attempted to organize the major principles of triangular therapy with a minumum of technical jargon. Case materials both from my own practice and from cases that I have supervised are included to illustrate the key points. In most chapters I have a sections on all of the things that can go wrong, with illustrations of how I had to learn from my mistakes as well as from my successes.

Naturally, much of the material in this volume is derivative. Credit is given where credit is due, but I have tried to avoid the overdocumentation that only demonstrates the erudition of the writer and impedes the progress of the reader. After all the credits are passed out, however, this remains a very personal document. It is my own distillation of the lore of triangular therapy as I have come to love and to practice it.

•

I

The Theory and Practice of Triangular Therapy

•   •

No couple, on the day of their marriage, can predict how their brave new enterprise will truly fare. Whatever their hopes, none can know until the event what comfort or despair, what celebration or humiliation lies ahead. What does seem certain is that many will fail, and the rest will distribute themselves on some sort of normal curve varying from the most lively and satisfying relationships to the most empty or conflicted.

It seems almost equally certain that, sooner or later, one or the other will seek help in dealing with the problems that arise in the relationship. Most will confide in a friend or relative; some in a physician or a lawyer or the clergy. Increasingly often, the person that they turn to will be a professionally trained marital therapist.

A marital therapist is someone who does therapy in triangles instead of dyads. It is a very different thing to see a husband *and* a wife—a relationship—as one's client than to see a single individual in that role.

This book is about therapy in the triangular context: how it is done, all the things that can go wrong, and some of the ways to salvage a case that has gotten out of hand, or gotten stuck, or headed off in the wrong direction. In Chapter 1 we introduce the general model of triangular therapy upon which the rest of the book is based. In Chapter 2 we examine a problem peculiar to the triangular situation, namely, how one maintains a symmetrical relationship with each client in the face of powerful temptations to join one or the other in an asymmetrical coalition. Chapter 3 deals with achieving therapeutic potency even when the couple works hard to subvert it.

Chapter 4 considers the issue of triangular diagnostics. When working with couples, the concepts developed in working with individual clients are simply inadequate to characterize what is causing the problem in the relationship. The relationship itself must be analyzed and treated according to its specific qualities.

This leads directly to the subject matter of Chapter 5: how goals are chosen, how divergent and sometimes conflicting agendas are dealt with, and finally how an implicit (or sometimes an explicit) triangular therapeutic contract is established between the therapist and the couple.

Detailed consideration of the various strategies of intervention will be delayed to the chapters in Part II.

Triangular therapists span the gamut of allegiance to particular metaphors, vocabularies, and techniques. In this book my effort will be to introduce as little special vocabulary as possible and to emphasize only the most fundamental and widely practiced techniques. Those with strong commitments to particular schools of therapy will surely wish to enlarge upon our presentation at several points and to supplement this book with appropriate readings in the preferred approach.

•

1

A Basic Model
for Triangular Therapy

•   •

The telephone rings.

"Good morning. This is the Crossroads Therapy Center. May we help you?"

"I hope so. Do you help straighten out messed up marriages?"

"What seems to be the trouble?"

"Everything! My husband and I just don't communicate. He doesn't support me with the children. We argue about money all the time. Sex is rotten. Now he's talking about leaving, and I think there may be another woman. Do you think there is any use seeing a counselor? Can you help us out of this mess?"

What happens next is the subject of this book.

Of course, only a minority of couples in trouble seek professional help of any kind. When they do seek it, they may be directed to a very wide range of practitioners indeed, even within the respectable community of professional therapists. Depending on how they conceptualize and present their problem and on the orientation of the person they initially consult, the treatment recommended could vary from the prescription of psychotropic drugs to body massage; from intensive long-term individual analysis to problem-focused short-term therapy.

Increasingly, however, a problem such as the one described in the opening phone dialogue is likely to be referred to a therapist who specializes in working on the marital relationship itself. It is this format involving a therapist and a couple that we have called *triangular therapy*.[1] This book explores the special qualities, strategies, and problems characteristic of this approach.

Therapists working with couples must, of necessity, deal with all the issues that might come up in individual therapy. But they also must come to grips with the peculiar dynamics of triangular relationships. Triads and their qualities have been studied from many points of view. Social psychologists such as Heider (1958) and Newcomb (1953); sociologists such as Simmel (1950), Caplow (1968), and O'Connor (1974); and family therapists such as Haley (1962), Minuchin (1974), Zuk (1971), and Framo (1981) have presented persuasive evidence that a three-sided relationship is different in many crucial ways from a dyad or a larger group.

In the traditional therapeutic dyad there are only two parties and one relationship between them to consider. In a triad there are three parties and *three* relationships to deal with. Each of the three members must attend not only to himself and to each other member as a person with needs, opinions, hurts, strengths, and so forth, but also to the quality of the relationship between each pair.

When the therapist (let us suppose she is a female) sits down for the first time with the couple who phones in about their problems, she is not free to focus solely on the content of the problems they brought in (communication, the children, sex, money, the other woman). She must also consider each of the six components of the triangle.

(1) *The husband.* What kind of a person is he? What are his strengths and weaknesses? What are his expectations

---

1. There are, of course, other possible therapeutic triangles, including a therapist and a parent-child dyad and even a single client and a pair of therapists. These configurations, however, will not be discussed in this book.

for marriage and therapy? His fears, his hopes, his prejudices?

(2) *The wife.* What background, attitudes, and behavior patterns does she bring to the marriage and to the session? What are her wants, needs, and responses?

(3) *Herself.* What in her own background or foreground may get in the way or be an asset in dealing with this couple?

(4) *The marriage,* the relationship between the husband and wife. What are its strengths and weaknesses and potentials? What rules govern it:
(a) from the husband's point of view,
(b) from the wife's point of view;
(c) from the external, objective point of view of the therapist?

(5) *The therapist's relationship with the husband:*
(a) from her point of view does she find him attractive? Intimidating? Seductive? Offensive?
(b) from his point of view is she seen as sympathetic? Competent? Unbiased?
(c) from his wife's point of view is she impartial? Overly sympathetic? A threat to the marital relationship? Lacking in understanding about what is really going on?

(6) *The therapist's relationship to the wife:*
(a) from the therapist's point of view;
(b) from the wife's point of view;
(c) from the husband's point of view.

Every experienced therapist knows that this is not just a list of all of the possible elements in a triangle. Each of the six, if ignored or mismanaged, can derail the therapeutic process.

The chief purpose of this book is to focus upon the special challenges and potentials that this triangular structure imposes upon the therapeutic process. Before that can be effectively achieved, however, it will be necessary to sketch out a basic model of the therapeutic process itself.

It is our observation that after generations of partisan conflict, a generally accepted view of the basic principles of therapy is emerging. Behind the variety of styles and rhetorics a consensus on the fundamentals is increasingly discernible. Different schools of therapy use different vocabulary to discuss the issues, but the set of issues tnemselves are becoming standardized.

Let us examine, then, the basic processes of therapy, of which triangular therapy is only a special case. We have chosen to organize our discussion around a model of therapeutic process first introduced into the literature by a sociologist rather than a therapist. We are partly motivated by the elegant simplicity and utility of the model, and partly it seems wise to avoid identifying too closely with the particular conceptual framework of any one of the contemporary schools of therapy.

THE BASIC THERAPEUTIC SPIRAL

Talcott Parsons, the noted Harvard social theorist of a generation ago, has provided the paradigm we wish to use (1955, pp. 39, 59). Parsons was interested in all aspects of social process and was particularly intrigued with the strong similarities he observed between the way parents socialize children and the way therapists resocialize clients. According to his analysis, in each case the process could be reduced to four basic steps that repeated themselves in a spiral as new levels of achievement were pursued.

Step 1. Noncritical Acceptance of the Client's Behaviors, Perceptions, and Feelings

It may seem paradoxical that a process that is designed to improve the couple's patterns of interaction should begin by accepting whatever is presented—even those very patterns that are most in need of being changed. The importance of this can be most readily appreciated when the alternatives are considered. Any display of shock, disapproval, annoyance, fear, or resentment on the part of the therapist is certain to make it more difficult for the client to be trustful and open. This principle is not restricted to marital therapists, but is a key element in the success of any professional who deals with people's problems, from the medical doctor to the tax consultant, and from the priest to the lawyer. In fact, the ability to extend nonjudgmental acceptance to a client's problems may be thought of as one of the principal marks that distinguish a professional from an amateur in any field. Acquiring this professional detachment is thus one of the first tasks of a professional in training. At its root is the philosophy that the therapist's role is to help the couple find ways to alleviate their marital pain and resolve their relational problems, not to judge the wisdom of their getting into their dilemma in the first place.

As anyone who has trained to become a therapist knows, it is not always easy to achieve this objective and accepting manner. If the presenting problem involves bizarre or violent behavior it may be especially difficult to stifle feelings of dismay or moral indignation. That is, pehaps, most difficult when the issue is one in which we have strong moral convictions. In some cases even experienced therapists may recognize a response in themselves that signals that they are not the person to work with this couple on this problem. A dignified referral is the best course in such cases.

One of the most common mistakes that beginning therapists are likely to make in their efforts to be accepting and nonjudgmental is to extend enthusiastic *approval* to the couple for some of their behavior. Although there may be a real place for therapeutic reinforcement of certain improvements later in therapy, this is a treacherous technique to use in the initial stages of a triangular relationship. Therapists who outspokenly approved certain patterns may naturally arouse the fear that they are equally passionate in their disapproval of other patterns. They have revealed themselves as judgmental and made it far more difficult for the clients to reveal less admirable qualities.

For example, in a recent supervisory session the author viewed a videotape of new trainee's first interview with a couple.

> *Husband:* So when I get fed up with her picking on me I just leave for a few hours.
>
> *New Therapist* (trying to be accepting): Well, that's probably a good thing to do when you get so upset—better than staying around and just getting more upset.

This response had the effect of aligning the therapist with husband (who wasn't even seeking her support of this behavior) and alienating the wife (who feels abandoned when he leaves like that).
A better response might have been:

Therapist: I see. You just get so upset that the only way to relieve the tension seems to be to get yourself out of there.

This response shows nonjudgmental acceptance of the client but does not imply approval.

Step 2. Unconditional Support of Each Client as a Person

The second step in Parsons's model is to extend unconditional support to each client as a person. This may occur concurrently with Step 1 but it is a quite different matter. Support involves a great deal more than merely accepting the client's behavior, feelings, or perceptions without criticism. The latter is, in its essence, passive, but active support requires the communication of concern and understanding. If Freud was the master of noncritical acceptance, Carl Rogers established the standard for unconditional support (1951). We will have more to say about his methods in a later section, but they consist chiefly of warmth and a receptive focus on the client's feelings.

Establishing Rapport as the Foundation for Intervention

Steps 1 and 2 taken together constitute what is often called building rapport or joining the clients. Parsons asserted (and clinical experience confirms) that no intervention will be successful until a foundation of support has been established. As the behaviorists sometimes put it, "you have to put money in the bank before you can make a withdrawal."
I am reminded of a couple I saw some years ago who were locked in a classic vicious circle. She was overly critical and demanding and he was sullen and totally resistant to all of her prodding. By the time I saw them this cycle had developed and

rigidified into a ritual of hostile, self-righteous attack on her side and passive-aggressive resistance on his. The pattern was so obvious that I decided to move immediately in the first session to subvert the cycle through a behavioral exchange exercise (this approach is explained more fully in Chapter 6). I asked her to choose from her long list of things he had failed to do since their honeymoon three or four things that she would really appreciate if he did them this week. She had a hard time with this. After so many years there was no list of three or four things that would make any difference. She wouldn't let him off the hook so easily. But I pushed her on it. Was he so perfect a husband that no improvement was possible? "Far from it!" Then there must be something he could do that would be an improvement. Eventually she came up with a list. Then I turned to him and said, "Now, what is on your list?" He said, "I get a list?" That was a new doctrine to him. He loved it. He savored it. (All of this made her very uncomfortable.) Then he said, "There is just one thing on my list. If you do it I'll do everything on your list. For one golden week—for seven glorious days—SHUT UP!" She objected that this abrogated her First Amendment guarantee to free speech, etc., etc., but he remained adamant. I said, "You can't do it, is that it?" She said, "I can do anything I set my mind to." So we concluded the deal. She wasn't too happy but he was ecstatic and could hardly get home fast enough to start cleaning up the yard and the other things on her list.

As they left I congratulated myself on how quickly I had got to the core of their problem and how smoothly I had overcome her resistance to the exchange. The next day her husband called. "I'm afraid we are going to have to cancel our appointment for next week." "Why?!" "My wife is in the hospital." "What happened?" "The doctor said that marriage counseling was bad for her."

A month later she called me up and read me off for having handled the session badly. I had not given her the chance to tell her story: her terrible childhood, her miserable marriage. I agreed to see her alone for this purpose. Only after I spent a month with her, receiving her pain and showing that I cared— only then would she permit me to begin to meddle in her marriage.

She was right and I was wrong. The principle is a universal
one. On one occassion I was discussing the issue with Gregory
Bateson, one of the great pioneering intelligences behind the
family therapy movement, and he related an incident that
occurred while he was observing a learning experiment being
conducted with dolphins. The design of the experiment
required that the animals be rewarded with fish only when
they performed the trick they were being taught; however, the
men who actually handled the dolphins were frequently
caught slipping them fish on the sly between experiments.
This infuriated the psychologists, who pointed out in the most
forceful way that such behavior confounded the experiment
and completely subverted their ability to draw correct
conclusions from this data. But nothing they said seemed to
work and the surreptitious feeding continued. One evening
Bateson was having a beer with one of the handlers, and he
leaned over and said, "Look, it makes no difference to me one
way or the other, but just between us, why is it that you fellows
refuse to follow the directions the psychologists give you? Why
do you continue to sneak fish to the dolphins when you know
how upset the directors will be if they catch you at it?" The
handler replied, "If I only feed them when they do tricks, I'll
lose them. They wouldn't do tricks for any amount of fish if
they didn't think I was their friend."

One of the most common mistakes therapists make (and
animal psychologists, too, it appears) is to attempt an intrusive
intervention without having first established rapport. On the
other hand, establishing rapport alone is not enough. At one
time some schools of therapy insisted that if therapists are able
to create a safe, nurturing atmosphere through their
acceptance and support, that is all they can or should do. The
couple will do the rest when freed to do so by the supportive
atmosphere. I believe it has been demonstrated, however, that
even the most client-centered, nondirective therapist is
selective in how he or she responds to various client inputs.
There is a consensus in the clinical community today that
therapy is not effective unless the clinician moves on to the
third and fourth steps in Parsons's model.

*Step 3. Intervention Designed to Change
the Clients' Behaviors, Perceptions, or Feelings*

At some point after rapport has been established, it is necessary to introduce a measure of strain into the triangular system. Some of the very patterns that were uncritically accepted initially must now become the targets for change.

The range of possible therapeutic moves at this point is only limited by the imagination of the therapist. One useful classification of approaches is to consider separately those that focus directly on behavioral changes and those that deal with changes in the clients' perceptions of each other and their relationship, and those that are concerned primarily with changing how each partner deals with feelings.

Each of these classes of intervention is the subject of a separate chapter in Part II. Here we note only that many books have been written promoting one or another of these approaches.

Changing Behavior

For many years the advocates of behavior therapy have pointed out that we are what we do. Their view is that marital relationships can only be considered improved if the behavior of each partner changes in desirable ways. They have developed techniques for describing current behavior and setting up programs for systematic behavior modification. Homework is almost always assigned. Some approaches involve helping couples to negotiate behavior change—as we tried to do, prematurely, with the couple who were enmeshed in the vicious circle. Communication and other interpersonal skills are taught.

Other therapists, although not adhering to the specifics of the behavioral approach, still are centrally concerned with producing change in the couple's behavior. They are simply pragmatists and believe that therapists ought accept no other criterion for success. A number of family therapists would count themselves in this camp.

Changing Perceptions

Therapists who concentrate on helping a couple to see the world differently would appear to accept the ancient proverb, "As a man thinketh in his heart, so is he." For example, the Rational Emotive school of therapy emphasizes that it is possible simply to revise the "tapes" that we play in our heads so as to avoid "horribilizing" and other self-destructive thought patterns.

Other therapists, such as Transactional Analysts, teach their clients a whole new metaphor for viewing life, complete with new vocabulary and constructs. Their belief is that through use of this metaphor clients may gain power over their lives (in this case by analyzing the parent, child, and adult parts of their psyche, and the various games they play to avoid authentic interaction).

Still others have developed great skill at using paradoxes and therapeutic double binds to achieve a reframing of the marital relationship. Finally, there are those who utilize dramatic imagery to capture the imagination and refurbish the conceptualizations of the clients.

Changing Feelings

The affective domain has also been a major focus of therapy of all kinds. Nondirective approaches help clients perceive and accept their feelings and differentiate them from the feelings and needs of others. Gestalt therapy uses physical posture, dream associations, talking to empty chairs—which are assigned to represent one's dead mother or one's "bad girl" or one's fear of crowds—all of which focus on the discovery and disposition of emotion. Many therapists rely heavily upon emotional catharsis (screaming, crying, hitting, and so on) as a means of reducing tensions and triggering growth.

An Eclectic View

It is our view that each of these three dimensions is important and that none can be overlooked in the training of a competant therapist. Behavior, perceptions, and feelings each influence the others as in Figure 1.1.

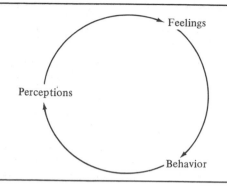

Figure 1.1

Changes in any one of the three inevitably lead to changes in the others. The task of the well-trained therapist is to know which of these approaches (or which combination of them) is most appropriate and effective for a particular couple at a particular point in their therapy.

In the process of dealing with these issues, the triangular therapist will also examine the rules that appear to govern the marital system. In the profession this is referred to as a second-order or metalevel analysis because it focuses *not* on the individual's behavior, perceptions, or feelings, but on the *structure* of the relationship between the two individuals. It is at this level that such pair issues as mismatched expectations, power struggles, and vicious circles come more sharply into focus.

Step 4. The Reinforcement of New Behavior, Perceptions, and Feelings

The final phase of Parsons's paradigm is concerned with establishing the gains achieved in the therapy. It is not enough to create a change in the system if one cannot find the means to make it stick. The object of triangular therapy, after all, is to bring the couple to the point where they can function well without further intervention from the therapist. The gains need to be internalized. In the optimal case the couple has learned not only the solution to the particular set of problems they came in with, but a new set of skills and perspectives with

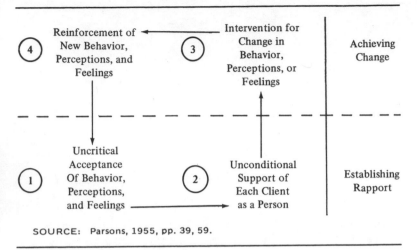

SOURCE: Parsons, 1955, pp. 39, 59.

Figure 1.2: Parson's Spiral of Therapeutic Process

which to resolve future problems as well. The old Chinese proverb—if you give a man a fish he has a meal, but if you teach a man to fish he has a means of providing meals for himself for the rest of his life—applies here.

In order to achieve this the couple may be followed for a few sessions, perhaps at increasing intervals, even after they have met their original goals. Perhaps the analogy may be made to wearing a cast for a period after the broken bone has been reset. Also, it is wise to leave the termination open-ended so that the couple feels free to return for a booster session or two if serious backsliding should occur several months down the road.

The four-step paradigm also provides for the possibility that after one round of objectives have been met, a couple may choose to go around the cycle again in pursuit of more advanced goals that they had not even considered in the original contract. Figure 1.2 summarizes Parsons's paradigm in graphic form.

Having outlined these basic processes in the therapeutic enterprise, we are prepared to proceed to a consideration of the special issues that are raised by the triadic structure of triangular therapy.

•

2

The Fine Art of Establishing
Triangular Rapport
The Principle of Symmetricality

•   •

It is agreed that the first task in any therapeutic endeavor is to establish rapport with the client. According to Parsons's model, this is a two-stage process involving the permissive acceptance of the client's nonfunctional behavior and simultaneously the active support of the client as a person. Well and good. But how does this work out if the client is a couple? How is it possible to be supportive of the wife while simultaneously being accepting of her husband's abusive behavior toward her? What does one do if one partner is jealous of the support you give the other or if one is constantly aligning himself or herself with the therapist as cohelper of his or her "disturbed" spouse?

Achieving triangular rapport must be viewed as the most crucial task of the initial stages of therapy. Years of experience have shown that people work most effectively, with the least defensiveness, when they perceive their relationship with their therapist to be warm, accepting, and nonthreatening. In this chapter we will consider the issues involved in establishing this type of relationship with two different and sometimes adversarial clients at the same time. We will look first at some of the situations that make it very difficult to maintain an even-handed symmetrical relationship and at some techniques for dealing with hard cases. Then we will consider all the things that can go wrong in the process of trying to use these techniques.

TASK:
TO ESTABLISH A SYMMETRICAL
RELATIONSHIP WITH THE COUPLE

The basic task of communicating acceptance and support for clients requires the same personal qualities and interpersonal skills in the triangular relationship as in the traditional dyadic situation. Listening well, showing respect for the clients, avoiding judgment or scorn or moral indignation—these are the foundations of rapport building in any situation. In triangular therapy, however, there is one additional issue of great importance: we may call it the *principle of symmetricality.*

Each client must feel *equally* accepted and supported. Experienced marital therapists find themselves constantly monitoring the symmetry of their relationships with the two partners almost without thinking about it. At a minimum he or she is aware of spacial symmetry, temporal symmetry, and, especially, moral symmetry.

Spacial Symmetry

The issue of where each member sits in relation to every other may seem trivial to the beginning therapist, and, in truth, this may not be the most crucial element in establishing the emotional closenesses and distances among the members of the triangle. Yet it is foolish to ignore the power of the symbolic statement made by spatial positioning. The wise therapist will utilize this as well as every other means at his or her disposal to establish and maintain balance in the relationships with each client.

If the arrangement of furniture in the office permits it, most therapists choose to sit in a position facing the couple and equidistant from them. If the relationships seem to be veering in one direction or the other, he or she may want to shift positions somewhat like a sailor leaning to adjust the balance in a crosswind. In our practice should we feel a husband becoming more and more distant and withdrawn as his wife recites an embarrassing inventory of his most humiliating vices, we may move physically closer to him or even touch him lightly to maintain equal contact.

Orientation is as important as actual distance in symbolic connectedness or its opposite. On the one hand we may become aware that one partner has engaged our attention and that we are facing that person and presenting a partial profile to the other. If such a posture is maintained for very long some clients, highly sensitized to the issues of acceptance and rejection, report feeling literally cold shouldered. This brings us to the question of time spent attending to each.

Temporal Symmetry

A therapist can ignore this application of the principle of symmetry only at his or her peril. By nature one member of a pair is likely to be more expressive than the other, but experience has taught that one partner should never be given the floor uninterrupted for more than a very few minutes. There are many techniques for passing the podium back and forth. The most natural is a simple shift in orientation. As partner 1 stops for a breath, the therapist may interrupt to reflect a feeling or otherwise show understanding, appreciation, and respect for his or her postion but then turn to the silent spouse and say something like, "I have been thinking that this must be very hard listening for you," or "I can hardly wait to hear your version of this," or "As hard as this was for her (him) I'll bet it wasn't easy for you either, ending up the villain in the piece."

This type of shift every few minutes keeps each person sure that their interests are being served and appreciated as well as their spouse's. Also, temporal symmetry is a major element in achieving moral symmetry.

Moral Symmetry

In many couples the issue of who is the most virtuous is on the agenda from the first minutes of the first session. Some come prepared to argue their case as persuasively as possible. They are skilled at making their own sins seem small, reactive, and mispercieved, while their partners' are manifestations of incredible and well-nigh unforgivable insensitivity, selfishness, and even cruelty. Often couples are well matched in their ability to put forward their own cases and to discredit their partners'. Their debating skills are polished and their arguments well rehearsed. Other couples come in badly matched in these skills, with one being a master of vituperation or sarcasm or virtuous recitation, and the other inarticulate, introverted, or stubbornly silent.

Still other couples come in with one partner so badly disadvantaged on the moral scale that there appears to be no hope for symmetry. He or she has recently done something violent or treacherous or disgraceful or crazy, while the spouse has been valiantly trying to cope with the resultant mess and has even sought out a therapist to help find a constructive solution to their ugly problem. Often enough the situation is made still worse by the one-up spouse virtuously confessing in the joint session that the guilty spouse resisted coming into therapy, expressing negative (and even profane) opinions about the whole therapeutic process, and making several unflattering observations about the character deficiencies of those who make their living off of other people's troubles. Such cases present a particular challenge to the principle of symmetricality. Yet, if some measure of symmetry is not achieved, in our experience the therapy has little chance for success.

Where the couple are well matched, but almost impossible to deter from their acrimonious debate, the problem is not really one of symmetry but of therapist potency, and is treated in the next chapter.

In the case where the adversaries are ill matched, however, it may be necessary for the therapist to become the spokesperson for the less articulate member. Lest one thereby violate the symmetrical premise in the very effort to achieve it, it is most important to give the more verbal partner compensatory strokes. For example, the therapist might reflect the articulate spouse's feelings first and then put words to the quiet partner's feelings. Since these must be deduced from minimal cues, one needs to be unusually careful to check out these perceptions as one proceeds. In some cases it may even be necessary to spend all or part of a session alone with the reticent spouse, teasing out the feeling that would be difficult to elicit in the presence of the active spouse. However achieved, becoming the spokesman for the silent partner in joint sessions can be a very effective move, provided one also shows support for the articulate spouse.

It sometimes happens that the less verbal partner would be quite willing to express themselves in the joint session if the more outspoken partner would let them. Every therapist must develop some nonoffensive means of getting the overly articulate participant to be quiet for a few minutes and let the other speak. This may be achieved by a polite request, accompanied perhaps with an expression of appreciation for the forward partner's talent at expressing him or herself so well. If that doesn't work, sometimes a lighthearted approach will. "Aha! Caught you interrupting again . . . four minutes in the penalty box," or whatever. A favorite of mine is to touch the over-eager partner with a light restraining hand. This shows them you have not forgotten them and wish to remain in contact, but you have them literally on hold. In especially difficult cases one can touch the client with one hand and hold the other in the air in a traffic control gesture. In our experience no one can talk through this double sign. The greatest test of therapeutic skill, however, comes when one of the partners has unjustly wronged the other. In such cases it is a real challenge to find the basis for sufficient moral parity to permit further work. Depending on the circumstances, several approaches are possible. While there may be no balance of guilt, there may be a balance of pain. One of the primary rules for establishing moral symmetry is: *focus on the pain each feels, rather than the pain each causes.* We think of a recent case in which a wife dragged her husband in for couples therapy after catching him with another woman. The wife was morally outraged at the infidelity, and deeply wounded. He was sullen and resentful at being brought in. The therapist said to the man, "You must feel just terrible. Your wife is furious with you. Your children are upset because she told them about it, you reputation is compromised, your self-image is shattered, and I'll bet even your girlfriend is giving you a hard time. Everyone has turned against you, and you are all alone." He started to sob and cry like an abandoned child. He literally wound himself into the office draperies to hide his shame and despair. This turn of events astonished his wife, who had been so preoccupied with her own feelings that she had not even considered the pain he might be in. The incident provided a foundation for approaching this problem as "partners in pain" rather than as saint and sinner or villain and victim.

We should make it clear that we do *not* subscribe to the doctrine that victims are always guilty coconspirators in their own betrayal. We see cases in which any fair judge would have to admit that there is simply no warrant for the hurt one partner receives from another. Often it turns out that the victim is merely a surrogate for some parent or former spouse whose hurtful behavior is now being vicariously repaid. In such cases it is helpful to both partners to explore these earlier experiences and their influences on current feelings and actions. As understanding increases, so does the opportunity to separate out those feelings that belong to the current relationship from those that belong elsewhere.

Despite these exceptional cases, the best rule of thumb is that there are two sides to every question and in nearly every case there is room for growth on both sides. It is always worth the trouble to find out from the villain the ways in which he or she is also the victim. Almost always there are criticisms, put-downs, withholding, and the like that helped trigger the villain's bad behavior. While the symmetry may not be perfect, at least each partner is acknowledged to be human with human motivations and responses and neither is assigned the role of angel or monster. This is sufficient to provide a foundation for joining as partners working on a set of interrelated problems rather than as accused and accuser.

When one stimulus to counseling is known to be a major sin of one partner against the other, it may be wise to split the session and see each one separately for at least a few minutes. This gives sinned-against partners a chance to vent their righteous indignation and hurt without their mates having to listen to it one more time. It also gives the sinners a chance to tell their side of the story without adding to the pain or anger of the aggrieved partners. Finally, it gives the therapist opportunity to extend sympathetic concern to each without appearing to take sides. Having established rapport with each separately it is easier to deal with them symmetrically in a joint session.

ALL THE THINGS THAT CAN GO WRONG

Murphy's Law is that if something can go wrong, something will go wrong. Certainly it has been our experience that there are a great number of things that can go wrong in attempting to establish symmetrical rapport with the couple. In this section we would like to consider some of the most troublesome.

Transference

Freud first introduced the concept of *transference* as a clinical issue of importance (1912, 1915). He observed that patients regularly transferred to their therapists feelings that had been characteristic of their relationship with their parents. It was as though the patients were trying to resolve in this new, safer setting, relational issues that were left over from their growing-up experience. Freud came to believe that the resolution of these transferences was the core of the therapeutic process. It has been suggested by some that transference is a less important issue in marital therapy than in traditional one-on-one therapy because the focus is on the couple's relationship with each other rather than the relationship of either with the therapist. Also, triangular therapy tends to be short-term and problem-focused rather than long-term and intense, thus further minimizing transference. Nevertheless, it is clear that a client's previous background can make quite a difference in how he or she relates to the therapist. Recently the author saw a couple in which the wife had been abused by her father, deceived by her husband, and insensitively treated by her minister. She felt that she had been extremely unfairly treated by God (a father figure in her theology). At the end of the first session the therapist summarized all this and said, "I wonder if you two ought to be seeing a male therapist?" She said, "I was thinking this myself. You seem to be a very wise man but to me you are still one of 'them' and I don't trust any of you." She was grateful to accept a referral to a female therapist, who found it much easier to establish a symmetrical relationship with this couple. We are not suggesting that the first therapist could not have succeeded. Some would probably insist that the woman's greatest need was to have a positive experience with a trustworthy male and that the therapeutic opportunity was ideally suited for that. That argument presumes a different therapeutic goal than the one this couple came in with. They were on the brink of an unhappy separation. They wanted to find whether they could achieve a viable relationship with each other. In that quest, it is our judgment, they could progress far more rapidly with a less-threatening female therapist who could establish a working rapport relatively quickly and get on with the task.

Each case needs to be handled on its own merits, but strong transference phenomena may frequently be most effectively handled by referring to another therapist or by adding a second therapist to help monitor the process.

Counter-Transference

Freud also identified a phenomenon that he called *counter-transference* (1912, 1915). It is the reciprocal of transference and refers to the feelings that therapists inappropriately transfer from their own relational past to current clients. One of the important elements in the training of therapists is helping them identify these feelings and to separate them from more appropriate and helpful response. Indeed every therapist, no matter how experienced, needs to be alert for signs that counter-transference may be getting in the way of establishing symmetrical rapport in a given case. For each of us there are certain categories of clients that are more problematic than others. In these cases it is particularly important to monitor the relationships with each client to be sure that our own unresolved relational issues are not intruding inappropriately into the therapeutic enterprise. When the problem is not resolved after several sessions, a referral to a colleague (with presumably different vulnerabilities) is strongly recommended.

Obviously there is an infinite variety of possible interactions between a clinician's emotional biography and his or her current work. It may be useful to note a few of the most troublesome and recurrent patterns, which I observe as a trainer of therapists (and in my own work also). Each of these will not be relevant for every therapist but it is likely that one or another may come close enough to stimulate self-analysis on this issue.

(1) Therapists with abusive, violent relationships in their background may find it especially difficult to deal with violent or bullying clients. The tendency is to respond (inwardly, at least) as we did when confronted with this in our own lives; that is, we may feel intimidated, placating, rebellious, or counter-abusive. We may also have difficulty in relating flexibly to the

abused spouse if she (or sometimes he) deals with the problem in ways that seem self-defeating or inappropriate to us. It may become far too important to have them adopt our own solution.

(2) Similarly, therapists who were neglected, treated unfairly, or taught that they were of no value as children may readily identify with an unloved, neglected, or downtrodden client. It is natural to feel compassion toward such a client and to respond with protective parental warmth and reassurance. Unhappily, it is equally natural to feel put off and judgmental toward the offending, insensitive, and hypercritical spouse. This presents a particular challenge that must be dealt with from the opening moments of the first session if an effective therapeutic symmetry is to be achieved.

(3) A special case of (2) deserves separate mention because of its potential for mischief. When the therapist's own emotional life is in disrepair and he or she feels a degree of loneliness, self-pity, and sexual deprivation, it may be particularly difficult to deal with an attractive member of the opposite sex who, in addition to having suffered abuse or neglect as a child, is also currently experiencing affectional and sexual deprivation at the hands of their partner. Typically the offending spouse refuses to come in or drops out of therapy after a session or two (an irrefutable indication that effective symmetrical rapport has not been achieved). Clearly the potential for sexual seduction of the therapist (or by the therapist—sometimes it is hard to distinguish one from the other) is very great in such a case. It follows that the therapist's ethical responsibility is to acknowledge his or her own vulnerability in such a situation and seek a referral or another professional or at least an ongoing consultation on the case with a trusted colleague. Failing that, the therapist has an obligation to impose sufficient structure and distance upon the relationship to permit therapy to occur. For example, it would be important to restrict contact with the the client to regular, prescheduled therapy hours in a professional setting, to avoid physical comforting, and so forth. It this advice sounds overly prudish or parental, I can only say that it is derived from a great deal of experience and observation over the years, and that many a career has prospered or floundered as a function of how this type of counter-transference is managed.

(4) Therapists who are competent, well-organized achievers themselves and who have spent some important part of their lives being frustrated by incompetent, unreliable, self-centered parents or spouses or children may have a lot of trouble with passive-aggressive clients. It is very easy in such a case to join with the more competant spouse in trying to reform the irresponsible and nonresponsive one. It is clear that if this trap is not avoided the therapy will fail, since it is as easy to defeat two reformers as one. The task, rather, is to get into the pain behind the passive defense and to establish an alternative style of dealing with it. This task is difficult enough even when unencumbered with the therapist's own "old business."

(5) Therapists who have grown up in the shadow of a sibling who was more beautiful, more accomplished, more talented, brighter, or more admired than they may have trouble with clients who exhibit those same qualities. Feelings of inadequacy, envy, or resentment may be hard to exorcise in such cases.

Clearly there is no limit to the number and variety of life experiences that have the potential of complicating the process of establishing symmetrical rapport.

Personal Issues

In addition to vigilence against the counter-productive potential of counter-transferences, the therapist must sometimes deal with his or her responses to clients who violate cherished values. A devoted feminist may have real trouble dealing compassionately with a totally unreconstructed chauvinist. Similarly, a therapist who has spent hours working with victims of sexual or physical child abuse or rape may have real difficulty in dealing with a client who molests children.

Prior Relationship with One Partner

It sometimes happens that a couple comes into therapy where one of the pair has already established a special relationship with the therapist. Perhaps it is a case of individual therapy developing into couple therapy. Perhaps the therapist has known one of the pair in a work or church or social setting. Whatever the circumstances that account for the existence of a prior relationship, it is clear that couple therapy requires a balancing of the triangle before effective intervention can take place. Probably the most obvious and best solution is to schedule one or more sessions with the less-connected member of the pair so as to establish a personal rapport and some degree of trust. In the process be sure to monitor the relationship with the other member lest he or she feel that an overcompensation has occurred, and now he or she is the one left out in the cold.

The final point of this section is this: When a couple comes to a marital therapist they have the right to expect to be accepted and supported in an even-handed manner. They have a right also to expect that the therapist has the capacity to set aside any personal issues of his or her own and to commit him or herself fully to the therapeutic enterprise. Whenever the clinician discovers that this process is not occurring for any reason, he or she is ethically obligated to do everything possible to overcome the problem. In the case where the barrier lies within the therapist, only two courses are professionally acceptable: (1) therapists may attempt to overcome their own impediments through consultation or in some other way, and (2) they may refer the couple to a colleague whom they trust to be free from this particular vulnerability.

When One Won't Come

How can you establish symmetrical therapy with a couple when one spouse won't come in? The answer is you can't. We would not go so far as to say that benefit to the marriage cannot occur unless you see both partners. That is manifestly untrue. Every experienced marital therapist has cases in his file in which one partner came in alone and accomplished a great deal to benefit the relationship.

Every one of us also has cases where it was clear from the start that individual therapy would almost certainly destroy the marriage. This occurs most frequently when one partner is demanding and abusive or at least insensitive and unrespon- sive, and it is the other partner who comes in alone. These situations lead to the victims getting more and more in touch with their own needs and their own worth. Their dissatisfac- tion increases and at the same time their courage to act upon it grows. Often they finally get up enough nerve to leave their unrewarding marriages.

Had both partners been seen, there is a substantial possibility that the offending spouse could have learned to soften up and open up and the marriage could have been preserved. It is our prejudice that it is almost always a more effective intervention when both partners are included in the therapy (whether in separate or conjoint sessions). How, then, can one induce a therapy-shy spouse to come in?

It may be confidently asserted at the outset that there is *no* strategy that will work with everyone and no combination of strategies that will work with certain committed hold outs. There are many reasons that people are reluctant to come with their spouse to a therapist. Several of these reasons are downright admirable and nearly all of them are at least comprehensible. Some people simply don't believe in therapy of any kind. They are convinced that people should take care of their own problems and not go running to someone every time something painful comes up. They may view professional help as a sort of emotional dole, a sign of personal incompetence and failure.

Others (sometimes with cause) have a profound distrust of the profession. They hear about therapists who mock values they hold sacred or who seduce their patients or who are crazy themselves, and they fear putting themselves into the clutches of such a person.

Many are afraid that they will be humiliated in front of a therapist, that their personal weaknesses will be relentlessly exposed, their intimate inadequacies displayed, their private sins held up to public judgment. They may (correctly or incorrectly) see being hauled off to a counselor as just another move by their spouse to place all the blame on them, while exonerating themselves.

Still others may feel that they are OK; it's their spouse who needs "fixing," so why should they have to come in?

Whatever the reasons for the resistance there are a number of strategies that counselors may use to try to establish a therapeutic triangle. Some simply insist that they see only couples and put the burden on the motivated spouse to get their partner in any way they can. We would never recommend it, but it is not at all uncommon for one partner to threaten or actually initiate divorce proceedings as a means of communicating to their spouse that their dissatisfaction is real. In effect, they say, "No therapy, no marriage."

Others, as one put it, "Just raised so much hell that it was easier to go to a counselor than put up with it."

Another strategy is for the therapist to see the willing spouse alone once and then phone the reluctant spouse and invite him or her to come in for one session. It is important that the reasoning be both motivating and honest. "I need you to help me to help your wife" is one example. Some are glad to take a personality inventory like the MMPI and come in for a joint feedback session. This sort or "glimpse into secret knowledge" has for some the fascination of X-rays or even of fortune tellers. Some can be motivated "to come and fill me in on the way things are from *your* point of view ... I keep feeling I am getting a distorted view of the way things really go at your house and I need to have confidence I am seeing the whole picture." Whatever the motivation for coming the first time, it is the therapist's job to make sure that the experience is a profitable one, that rapport is established, and, if possible, that a contract for conjoint therapy is achieved.

•

3

The Fine Art of Establishing
Triangular Support
The Principle of Therapist Potency

•   •

It has been noted that only when the therapist has established an effective working relationship with each member of the pair can he or she become an effective agent of change. Put differently, only when effective symmetrical rapport is established with the couple does the therapist acquire the power to intervene successfully. In the last chapter we dealt with some of the problems that arise when one partner is much easier to connect with than the other. But in some cases the challenge is rather how to connect with the couple at all. Some husbands and wives are so tenaciously involved in the power struggle with each other that the therapist can scarcely find an entry point. As one therapist trainee put it, "There was so much energy in the vicious circle that I was afraid if I tried to stick something in the spokes to slow it down, I'd break my arm."

In the most difficult cases it almost seems that despite the fact they have come seeking help, couples conspire together to defeat any help that is offered. It is as though they dare the therapist to try to change their established, destructive exchange.

Often the challenge to the therapist as to who is to control the marital interaction and also the sessions is very open and direct. For example, "Our minister suggested that the basic answer to our problems was more positive thinking. I believe we'd get further if we didn't dwell so much on the negatives," or "Look, we're not paying you to sit there and commiserate with us, we want some answers," or "Why do all you shrinks think everybody is angry. I'm not angry! I'm disgusted! I'd love to meet a shrink who could talk to you for five minutes without deciding the problem was that I'm angry. The problem is that I'm married to a slob. Five minutes in our house and you'd *smell* what the problem is."

It is clear that whether therapists find themselves impotent observers of a life-and-death struggle over who is right, or whether they themselves are drawn into the conflict over who is in charge, no effective therapy can take place until they have established the power to turn the therapeutic process into a constructive course. The fundamental purpose of achieving rapport is that only in this way can the therapist be potentiated.

TASK:
TO OVERCOME NEGATIVE COALITIONS

One of the most difficult challenges for a therapist is what to do with a couple who will not stop arguing long enough for any work to go forward. O'Connor has labeled these types of power struggles *negative coalitions* against therapeutic change (1974). His research with inexperienced therapists found that it was possible to predict with great accuracy in the first session what the outcome of therapy would be. If the couple were permitted to dominate the session with negative exchanges it was almost certain that six weeks later the case would have either terminated unsuccessfully or be stuck in an unproductive weekly repetition of the first session. The only exceptions were three cases where, after failing to achieve control of the first session, the fledgling therapists were wise enough to find a strategy for breaking up the coalition in the second session. In two cases the husband and wife were seen separately for a couple of sessions. The purpose was to establish one-on-one rapport with each so that each would agree separately to observe new rules of exchange when the joint sessions were resumed.

In the other case a second therapist was added to the session. This beefing up of the therapeutic troops was a successful strategy in this instance. The client couple were able to defeat the efforts of one therapist to intervene in their contest of wills, but two were too many for them.

Another strategy is to use the technique known as *paradoxical reframing*. In a later chapter the rationale and applicability of this technique will be more fully addressed, but its potential may be judged from this example. The author was visiting a training program on the East Coast and had agreed to do a demonstration for the staff and trainees. It was arranged that he should interview a couple one of the trainees had been seeing for 27 weeks without much progress. On a hunch he asked for a package of 3 × 5 index cards as he went into the session. Hardly had he been seated and introduced himself when the couple started on their routine of attack and counterattack. They were well matched and very talented at it, never missing a beat as they slung accusations back and forth. The therapist began to award a card to each person as they made a point. The rapid-fire pace of the match may be appreciated from the fact that it took only 25 minutes to distribute the entire stock of 100 cards. Finally, with only one card left, the therapist shrugged his shoulders, tore it in half, gave one-half to each and said, "I'm sorry, but I'm out of cards." The wife, who had been watching his activity with one eye (the well-rehearsed exchange with her husband occupied only part of her attention) said, "What's with the cards?"

"I was awarding each of you points to see who was best, but your are both *very* good, and I suspect your have virtually the same number of cards."

Both blushed with pleasure at the unexpected compliment, and she said, "Aw, really? Don't all couples who come in for therapy argue like this?" "Some try," the therapist assured her, "but you two are world class. I doubt if, in my entire career, I have run into another couple with more talent in this area than you two."

Recognizing that they were being teased as well as complimented, the husband said, "Look, we're here to get help, but don't you need to hear about our complaints before you can do anything for us?"

The therapist asked, "How many weeks have you been doing this here at the center?" "Twenty-seven." "I see. And how many more weeks were you planning on doing this before you got down to work?" "Well . . . like what else could we do that would work better?" "Ah . . . let's talk about *that!*"

The couple spent the second half of their hour in a far more profitable exchange of views about what they might do to make things better between them.

We are not suggesting that this particular card gimmick is of any special value. I have never used it before or since this particular incident, but it served on that occasion to redefine the couple's conflict as a highly skilled competition between two well-matched, worthy opponents. It was a game, not the real thing. When it was time to get down to work, they had to set the game aside until they had the time for it again.

Whatever the strategy employed, the task that must be achieved is to establish a problem-*solving* rather than a problem-*rehearsing* agenda for sessions—to convert opponent to teammate.

A final strategy, which we shall also return to in later chapters, might be called the utilization of *therapeutic sadness*. At the end of a session in which nothing good has happened despite the therapist's efforts to reframe the exchange, he or she might, quite honestly, say something like, "I feel so sad, listening to you two bruise and hurt each other. Each of you have suffered enough. You need love and support from your partner and you have love and support to give . . . but somehow it just never quite happens. Instead you get bogged down in this awful, destructive quarreling, while on the inside you are both starving to death. You came to me for help out of this trap and I haven't succeeded in finding a way to help you. I really feel terrible about it. So much love, so much potential . . . and yet so much pain and so little profit."

Sometimes a simple dose of this is enough to help a couple to reevaluate their destructive patterns. In one case the author had found no other approach worked for several weeks. Finally the wife wrote a letter, the main thrust of which was, "We have been coming here for several weeks now and paying you good money and nothing has changed. He is still doing the same things and I am too. All you ever do for your money is tell us how sad you are that things are not better. Well, the hell with it, we can't afford it if that's all you are going to do. We'll keep our appointment on Wednesday but we have agreed that will be our last one." Frankly, the therapist felt terrible on receipt of the letter. Their complaint was just. That *was* all he had done for several weeks . . . that and listen helplessly as they crucified each other. When they came in on Wednesday he said (trying to put the best possible face on it), "I appreciated your letter. I'm afraid I agree with you that it is not profitable for you to keep coming with nothing happening. Would you like a referral to someone else or what?"

The wife interrupted this last line with, "Oh, I'm so ashamed that I sent that letter! I know it wasn't your fault. Right after I sent it we sat down and *tried* really hard to communicate in a different way. It wasn't easy, but we kept at it. It took us three hours to get one issue settled and we kept slipping back into the old way but we finally made it. We know we need help and we're ready to work."

You can imagine the relief the therapist felt to be reassured once again that therapeutic sadness is a powerful intervention when other more direct approaches fail. In my opinion it would have been a very bad strategic error to have given up the contest one week sooner.

But whatever the strategy employed, whether separate sessions in which new rules are negotiated one-on-one, or bringing in additional help in the form of a cotherapist, or paradoxical reframing, or therapeutic sadness, or some other strategy ... some means must be found to replace the problem-rehearsing power struggle with a problem-solving style of interaction. The adversary relationship of the negative coalition must be replaced by a coworker relationship in which the therapist has the potency he or she needs to pursue therapeutic goals effectively.

TASK:
DEALING WITH THE COUNTER-INITIATIVE
OR POWER MOVE

Even more difficult than the couple engaged in a negative coalition is the couple with one member who challenges the therapist directly, putting him or her on the defensive, and attempting to gain control of the session. There are many ways that clients may do this—challenging statements made by the therapist, refusing to follow his or her suggestions, or to confirm his or her interpretations of what is going on, what needs to happen next, and so on. In no way are we suggesting that the therapist is always right and that any challenge is ill motivated and contentious. Sometimes the therapist is off on the wrong foot and needs to be challenged. We *are* suggesting, however, that until the therapist can establish working control over the session, he or she is denied a key move in all successful therapy, the intervention for change.

To illustrate the counter-initiative or power play and how it might be dealt with, consider the following case.

The husband was large and had an intimidating scowl on his face. As he entered the office, he commented that it was "surprisingly shabby for this sort of practice."

The therapist considered a light rejoinder but decided to let it pass, and after getting everyone seated opened the session with a fairly standard question, "Well, now ... what brings you?"

Couples may respond to such an initiation in a variety of ways. Sometimes one takes a list out of purse or pocket, sometimes one turns to the other and says something like,

"This was your idea, why don't you tell the doctor why we're here." Sometimes, if it happens to be an unusually contentious couple, such as those discussed in the previous section, they may both jump in at once and try to tell their side of things. In this case, however, the husband took charge immediately. In a strongly assertive voice he said, "Before we get into what brings us here, Doctor, I'd like to find out something about your training and philosophy of therapy."

This is, of course, a legitimate request at the content level and if the metalevel message were noncontentious, the best strategy would clearly be simply to answer the question. In this case, however, it appeared to be an attempt to assume control of the session. It shifts the focus from the couple's problem to the therapist's qualifications, and it directly challenges the therapist's opening move to set the agenda. In this case the therapist wisely responded to the style of questioning rather than to the content. She said in a mild voice, with a slightly amused expression on her face, "My goodness . . . do you usually get good results in life by attempting to intimidate the people that you meet?" At this point the wife said, "He does. That's his whole approach to life. To me, to the kids, to the people who work for him. If he can make everyone afraid of him, he doesn't have to deal with their needs." He did not give up the strategy at this point, but the initiative had shifted, and it was possible for the therapist to proceed with the session instead of falling into a defense of her training, philosophy, and competence.

Although there are a number of ways a therapist might respond to this type of initiation, in general they might be grouped into three categories: co-opting the client's agenda, confronting the client directly (the strategy used falls into this category), and reframing the client's power move so that it is convincingly labeled as something other than a power move. For example, given this client's confrontive grab for control, the following are possible responses in each category:

(1) *Co-opting* the client's agenda: "That is an excellent question. I wish more people with marital problems had the wisdom to evaluate their therapist's competence

before committing themselves to therapy. I was trained
. . . (and so on). Have you any other questions? Good. Now,
what brings you?"

(2) *Confronting* the client (note: this is a dangerous maneuver since it can lead to a spiralling power struggle,
but in some cases it can be very effective): "I see that you
are used to taking charge of situations. Your question is
a good one and I will be happy to answer it later but first
(to the spouse) tell me how it is being married to such a
strong, assertive character?"

(3) *Reframing* the client's move: "I don't blame you for
wanting to put off telling me why you are here. It is very
painful to have to confront such issues in front of a
stranger. Well, let me tell you about my training and by
the time I'm finished perhaps you will feel more comfortable in discussing the issues with me."

Any of these responses has a good chance of recapturing the
initiative for the therapist. Of course these examples reflect
the personal style of the author. Other therapists would
doubtless come up with different examples of each type of
response.

There are many ways that a client may challenge the
leadership of the therapist. On one occasion a male therapist
had spent the first session taking a history of a rather painful
marital relationship. Among the key issues was the husband's
abuse of alcohol and the wife's continual pressure on him to
stop. Just as it was time to end the session, the wife said crisply
and with some finality, "Frankly, I can't see the value of your
going into all of this. You'll never be of any real help to us if you
don't get him to stop drinking. You can spend all the time you
want on these other issues. He'll love that. But you'll simply be
wasting your time and ours."

At the beginning of the next session the therapist
responded with a confrontation that also had a bit of the flavor
of co-opting the client's agenda. He acknowledged the reality
and legitimacy of the wife's pain around the issue of her
husband's drinking. He also validated her observation that her

husband seemed relieved when the conversation veered to some other topic. But he then explained that from his point of view the alcohol consumption was embedded in a broader and more complex pattern of marital destructiveness and that if they chose to stay with him they must accept working on the entire system, not just one piece of it, however painful this piece was.

He was able to convince them that this approach was reasonable and consistent with all the best professional opinion. The matter kept cropping up, but he was able to deal with it successfully each time because he was clear on his own philosophy and persuasive in his presentation of it.

ALL THE THINGS THAT CAN GO WRONG

Therapists whose life experiences have made them diffident or self-doubting are liable to have difficulty in wresting control of the initial sessions from self-confident, assertive clients. They are also more likely than others to be defeated by stubborn negative coalitions. O'Connor (1974) was able to demonstrate this principle quantitatively. Using the Ego Strength scale of the MMPI he found that therapeutic success or failure could be reliably predicted from the relative scores of the members of the triangle. Only when the therapist had a decisive edge did the clients move toward their goals. When one or both of the clients had higher scores than the clinician the whole process inevitably got stuck and stayed stuck unless special corrective measures were employed.

The chronic lack of self-confidence is so great a handicap that, in our view, trainees with this problem ought to be discouraged from seeing clients until they have remedied it. Individual or group therapy or assertiveness training are often effective in a reasonably short time if the damage is not too great.

Since the problem is relative rather than absolute ego strength, virtually every therapist must deal with the problem at some time. When facing a couple with more negative energy than they can cope with therapists have recourse to several corrective strategies: (1) they can refer the case to a particularly charismatic colleague; (2) as suggested earlier in the chapter they can break up the coalition and attempt to establish rapport with each partner separately (divide and conquer); (3) they can shore up their positions by seeking consultation, supervision, or a cotherapist; (4) they can devise a strategy for utilizing the client's strength against the negative coalition.

This last approach, similar to the tactics of a judo master, pits the therapist's *skill* against the client's strength, rather than permitting a nose-to-nose contest of power. For example, if one spouse is particularly dominating and intrusive, one strategy is to co-opt them into the therapeutic enterprise by assigning them the task of coming up with viable alternatives to their present dilemma. It is amazing to see how even insensitive, antipsychological individuals can rise to the challenge and come up with sensible and even-handed solutions, which they never would have accepted if they had not thought of them themselves. Once co-opted into the therapeutic enterprise, of course, they become available for still further modifications of their interpersonal styles.

In effect, this is a *paradoxical* tactic—giving up power to achieve power. In later chapters we will look at other examples of paradoxical intervention, all of which share this judolike quality. Through such means a skillful therapist can often succeed with even the strongest-willed and intimidating clients.

Premature Leap to Intervention

There is an equal and opposite trap to the one we have just discussed. Some therapists, far from feeling intimidated by a particular couple, are able to establish control of the session almost immediately. It is a strong temptation in such cases to make a premature leap to intervention before establishing a sufficient reservoir of good will.

Perhaps the most dramatic case of that in my own practice occured when I saw a couple who had been married for only about a year. It was the second marriage for both and they had adopted the role of rescuer and rescuee (with the wife in the rescuer category). He was constantly threatening to kill himself because he was such a "nothing" and she was too beautiful and good for him. With little provocation he would leave the house and go wandering around the streets in the middle of the night until she came and found him. On one occasion he leapt from a moving car and nearly got killed in traffic.

In the first session she dominated the conversation (despite my efforts to establish symmetry), outlining their problem and emphasizing that they desperately needed immediate help (they had been to a therapist who only listened and he had been no help at all). I obliged them by helping them negotiate some behavioral exchanges. The next week I was not able to schedule them due to a family crisis of my own. The third week they came in fairly glowing. Everything had gone wonderfully She was especially grateful at the miraculous change. He agreed with her but looked, somehow, less enthusiastic about it all. Two nights later I got a call in the middle of the night. With little provocation he had fired a gun at her and threatened to kill both of them. The police intervened in the therapy.

In my opinion, that would have been far less likely to occur if I had resisted her pressure for active help until I had established a more solid connection with him. Clearly, he was a very disturbed man and I ignored the clinical cues because both the wife and I wanted to get things moving right away.

I believe it is a universal law of therapy that you cannot successfully introduce change into a marital system before you have established a meaningful connection with each of the partners. If there is a single error that bright, self-confident, assertive therapists are likely to make it is to pace the therapy faster than the client's trust permits. Particularly when the patterns are deeply rooted, as in this case, careful attention to rapport-building is at the core of success.

In sum, the burden of this chapter and the last is that the first task of triangular therapy is to establish symmetrical, effective rapport with the couple. Unless this is accomplished nothing else constructive is likely to happen.

•

4

Diagnosing Couples' Problems

•   •

Diagnosis is a term most often associated with medical practice. In that context it refers to the identification of a disease through analysis of presenting symptoms. Because of that association, some object to its use is discussing marital therapy. They are offended at the implication that relational difficulties may be equated with "diseases." We use the term rather in its root sense of *differentiation among conditions.* Whatever one's conceptualization of marital interaction, it must be agreed that all couples are not alike and that all problems cannot be resolved in the same way. The determination of what is required by this couple with this problem at this time is what we mean by diagnosis.

Every diagnostic system includes three types of element. First, there must be some set of ways of characterizing couples' problems. Second, there must be some repertoire of possible therapeutic responses to the couple's problems, and finally, there must be some set of rules for linking particular problems to particular responses.

Over the history of the field many such sets of diagnostic systems have been put forth. It would not be profitable to attempt to review all of them. Rather we will attempt to outline a fairly simple diagnostic model. Our hope is that those trained in other vocabularies and systems will find this approach basic enough to be easily translatable into most other diagnostic idioms.

Before proceeding to the main task, it may be useful to consider briefly certain attitudes and practices that, in our view, are subversive of effective diagnosis and treatment. We think of them as the follies and fallacies of diagnosis.

FOLLIES AND FALLACIES OF DIAGNOSIS

First, is the *Procrustean folly.* In Greek mythology Procrustes was an innkeeper whose passion was to provide every traveler with a bed that exactly fit his measure. Since he owned only one, nonadjustable iron bedstead, the only available remedy was to stretch short travelers and trim long ones. Some therapeutic styles approach this degree of rigidity. The commitment to a particular mode of treatment is so complete that every couple is forced into the same mold regardless of their need or circumstances. This effectively eliminates the need for diagnosis, although to give credit where credit is due, many such therapists do exercise at least the primitive diagnostic procedure of screening out some couples as unsuitable for their program.

There are many reasons why some may be helped even by the most inflexible approach. Some, whether by chance or pre-selection, will find a workable match between the program and their needs. Others will improve simply because they are now focusing attention on their marriage (the so-called *placebo* effect). Still others will be mobilized by the inappropriateness of the treatment to administer more on-target corrections themselves. But it must also be acknowledged that many who are treated by the "one-note" therapist will find they have wasted their time, their money, and their hopes. An unhappy few are likely to find their problems actually aggravated by the experience.

A second, less extreme, but similar problem we have labeled the *true believer fallacy.* The short history of our field has produced more than its share of strong, attractive, charismatic innovators. A substantial number of therapists are true believers in the approaches of one of these superstars. They identify themselves with them, and adopt the vocabulary, the strategies, and even the personal mannerisms of their models. These cases of discipleship need not always result in more Procrusteanism. Some of these charismatic leaders have developed comprehensive systems of diagnosis and treatment, capable of dealing with a broad spectrum of problems. Our concern is that, as a matter of loyalty, true believers are prepared to ignore or even denounce any other therapeutic perspective or treatment strategy. By contrast, we are persuaded that the best training for therapists must be founded upon an enlightened eclecticism that is open to inputs from any quarter. Any other approach systematically excludes important issues from consideration and thereby risks cheating the client couple of the best possible approach to their problem.

At the other extreme of the rigidity-flexibility continuum lies what we think of as the *humanist fallacy.* This is premised upon the beguiling principle that since no two couples are alike and, indeed, no single couple is static in its structure and function from session to session or even from moment to moment, it is foolish to attempt any form of diagnosis. Rather, the therapist must flow with the process, being as infinitely various in his or her responses as the couple is in their interaction.

This view is so attractive and even self-evident that it easily seduces one into overlooking its fatal flaw. It has been our observation that the typical therapeutic repertoire is far from infinitely varied. We have seldom seen a therapist who knew more than a handful of ways to respond to a couple's problems. He or she may know three or four ways to show support (nodding, smiling, reflecting, attending) and three or four ways of confronting (giving behavioral assignments, reframing, etc.), but that is the full variety of the available responses. Given such a finite variety of available responses, only an equally finite number of rules is required to determine, for example, when it is most appropriate to nod and when it is most appropriate to reframe. It follows that the infinite variety of inputs from the couple needs somehow to be reduced to a handful of categories, each linked to one of the responses in the therapist's repertoire so that he or she knows when to do what. If a couple behaves in a way that doesn't come under one of the rules, it must be dealt with in a "does not compute" or "dump" category. That is, it must lead to some nontherapeutic response such as a client-therapist power struggle or early termination.[1]

The final diagnostic folly that we wish to note might be called the *folly of terminal diagnosis*. It is evident that to be of any value, a diagnostic categorization must be linked by some rule to a helpful response. One of the reasons that many couples cannot solve their own problems is that they tend to utilize a set of terminal (that is, incurable) diagnoses. They see their problems as due to their never having been meant for each other, or to their spouse's character defects (lazy, stupid, immature, crazy, frigid, oversexed, irresponsible, selfish, etc.), or to some baleful external influence (her mother, his drinking buddies, that other woman). All of these, of course, are known to be incurable conditions. The therapist's task is to rediagnose the pattern of interaction so that the new categories suggest solutions. We call this *motivational diagnosis*. It is the only kind that is of benefit to the couple.

One study of therapist trainees (Pulliam-Krager, 1974) observed that when inexperienced clinicians found themselves stuck and frustrated in a case, they routinely resorted to terminal diagnosis as a means of rationalizing their failure. Ignoring the relational diagnostic schema they were being trained in, they fell back upon such labels as "psychopathic,"

---

1. *This is the well-known law of requisite variety, which is derived directly from systems theory. This law requires that the number and variety of inputs into a system cannot exceed the number and variety of rules in the system for linking them to outputs, and that the number and variety of outputs also cannot exceed the number and variety of rules in the system.*

"paranoid," "masochistic," and even "s.o.b.," and "flaming bitch"—all terminal categories. A more profitable strategy would have been to reassess the situation and, with the help of a supervisor, determine what might be more effective diagnoses and treatments.

THE LEVEL OF DIAGNOSTIC FOCUS: CONTENT VERSUS PROCESS

The first task is to decide whether to focus on the *content* of the couple's exchanges or on the *process*. By content we mean the substantive issues they bring in, such as sex, money, the children, the in-laws, his temper, her housekeeping, his hitting her, her cheating on him, and so on. By process we mean the style of interaction around these issues such as power struggles, vicious circles, triangulation with a third party, destructive games, systematic misperception, and so forth.

One of the most significant developments over the history of relationship therapy has been the steady shift of emphasis from content to process. The contemporary clinician is far less likely than his predecessors to diagnose a couple's problem as poor money management and respond by teaching them to use a budget. It would be more likely, these days, to come up with a diagnosis of, for example, mismatched scripts aggravated by adversarial interpersonal style. Such a diagnosis implies specific tasks that the therapeutic triangle must address. In the process of exploring the discrepancies in their scripts for handling money and attempting new styles of negotiating the differences, the couple might well solve their money management problem. More importantly, they would learn a more effective approach to the solution of any problem.

In the same way, a contemporary therapist, confronted with the symptoms of a husband's impotence or a wife's sexual nonresponsiveness, is likely to approach the problem as a breakdown in marital understanding and communication rather than focusing narrowly on the sexual difficulty itself.

In the literature, focus on the content of the interaction is often referred to as *first-level* analysis, while a focus on the process of interaction is referred to as analysis on the *second* or *metalevel.* Thus one may read of *second-order change* (Watzlawick, Weakland, & Fisch, 1974) or of utilizing a *metaperspective* (Watzlawick, Beavin, & Jackson, 1967), indicating that the focus is on the process rather than substantive concerns. One of the first tasks of a contemporary therapist, then, is to analyze the interaction of the client couples with compassion and sensitivity, and to come up with a diagnosis that implies corrective action at the process level. The underlying assumption is that if the couple relates well to each other on a process level, they can handle their own content problems without the supervision of a therapist. On the rare occasions when a therapist is consulted by a husband and wife who relate well on a metalevel, it is generally a one- or two-session case. After dealing with some blind spot or misunderstanding, it is generally found that no further intervention is needed.

The skill required for a second-level analysis is not easily taught in a book. In our experience it is learned best by watching others do it and by getting corrective feedback from a supervisor as one attempts to do it oneself. Some seem to have a real talent for it, which we suspect was developed in dealing with the complexities of their own family interactions while growing up. Others, for whatever reason, seem to be stuck at the concrete level. They can never seem to get past the content of the stories the couples are telling about what happened last week, or "what he always does to me," or "what she never remembers." The dynamic analysis of why they are telling stories, and what part they play in the perpetual game between them, is not perceived and therefore never becomes part of the therapy.

One way clinicians can tell that they are operating at the wrong level is that they keep hearing the same (or equivalent) stories over and over in sessions, but nothing seems to happen to the relationship.

A MODEL FOR SECOND-LEVEL DIAGNOSIS— THE DISENGAGED-ENMESHED CONTINUUM

If our task is to develop a way to categorize couples that is sensitive to the style of interaction between them rather than to the content of their conflict, it seems to us best to start with what might be thought of as the gross anatomy of the relationship. That is, are the couple very tightly bound so that everything one does has an immediate impact on the other, or are they very loosely bound with many barriers between them so that it is extremely difficult for either to have any impact on the other?

This dimension has been called the *enmeshed-disengaged continuum* (Minuchin, 1974). Couples at one end are so tangled up in each other's lives that everything happening to one has immediate repercussions with the other. It is as though they constituted a single unhappy organism without either partner having a clear identity separate from the other. At the other end are those couples with so few bonds connecting them that there is little meaningful communication and few shared experiences. It is as though they have achieved a nearly complete immunity from each other. Although there is a true continuum, with couples occupying every position from one end to the other, in clinical practice we are more likely to see those from either extreme. It appears that those in the middle manage somehow to deal with their problems without professional help. There is a third group that is likely to show up, however, and that is those with dramatic asymmetry in their degree of reactive involvement. In such couples one partner may seem totally wrapped up in the marriage, while the other partner seems to have little concern for or attachment to their spouse.

As might be imagined, each of these three types of relationships is likely to bring different problems into therapy.

The Enmeshed Couple

It is easy to identify the enmeshed couple. Everything one partner says or does gets a reaction from the other. It may be a case of symmetrical give and take, as with a couple who argues constantly in an equally matched, nonstop marathon throughout the session. It may be complementary where one yells and the other cries, or one talks nonstop while the other stubbornly refuses to express their feelings. In either case it is very hard for the outsider to break into the system or to have any impact on it.

Enmeshed couples vary in the way they express their relationship. For example, the partners may speak for each other so that when you address one the other responds, explaining what *our* feelings are about the matter. Another common indicator is the couple's having to glance at each other every time a new subject comes up to make sure that it is OK to proceed. Gradually the therapist may discover that there are whole subject matter areas that are off limits, such as her drinking, or his former affairs, or their ten-year-old daughter's bed-wetting.

Enmeshed families are rule ridden, but it is almost always one of the rules that the rules must not be discussed. We are not suggesting that this collusion is fully conscious and explicit (although sometimes it is), but we are suggesting that it is powerful in its effects. In such a case the easiest way to deduce the rules is by observing them in operation. For confirmation, all we need to do is challenge one. For example,

Therapist: Tell me something good about your wife.

Husband: I can't think of anything.

Therapist: I see. I suspected you had a strict rule about that. That explains why you are so negative about her when she is present but less when she is absent.

Husband: I wouldn't say it was a rule. It's just that sitting here with her I can only think about how many ways she has screwed me and it's hard to forget all that and say something nice. I don't feel anything nice about her.

Therapist: Hm. OK. Shut your eyes and take some time to put those feelings aside. Now, as objectively as possible, think of something about your wife—anything at all that is positive.

Husband: Well, (long pause) . . . I suppose some people would say she was friendly but she don't act friendly to me so I don't see what difference it makes.

Therapist (With admiration in voice): You are really good about keeping your rule. I put you under quite a bit of pressure just now to break your rule and you didn't give an inch. That's not easy. I'm impressed. You really have a lot invested in not giving her any positives. It seems to be tied to your integrity or something—your loyalty to yourself.

Husband: Yeah . . . OK . . . I guess that's right. After all the dirt she has did to me it would be like selling myself out to sit here and say how wonderful she is. I don't deny she may have some good points, but I got no reason to dwell on 'em.

Notice that this is a metadiagnosis. It focuses on the rules that govern the interaction between them rather than on the interaction itself. By contrast, a first-level diagnostic statement might be,

Therapist: I see that your wife has hurt you so badly that you can think of nothing good to say about her.

Such a statement would be likely to elicit a response such as,

Husband: You're damn right! You'd feel the same if you'd had to put up with all the crap I put up with these last few years (etc.).

In our clinical experience the second-level issue (the rule) is more open to change than the first-level issue (the justification of the hurt).

Among the most frequently observed patterns of enmeshed interaction are power struggles (that is, struggles to see who is in charge of various parts of their joint life) and vicious circles. The two are closely related, but vicious circles are especially interesting dynamically. Unlike the simple power struggle, in a vicious circle each partner is trying to solve the problem, but the method he or she is using makes the circle spin faster rather than slowing it down or stopping it. Each partner's strategy is maintained despite its manifest failure by a dark fantasy that things would be much worse if any other strategy were attempted. In effect, each partner ignores the actual results of their strategy and pleads their intentions (which are always noble). Vicious circles are further distinguished by their severe symmetry. The two partners contribute equally to the circle and either could stop it if they disengaged from it (allowing for a few further turns from sheer momentum).

For example, it is common for students in therapy training programs to get very involved with experiencing and expressing their feelings, opening up deeper levels of communication, and so forth. In their enthusiasm for their new vocabulary, insight, and emotional freeing up they sometimes rush home to try to free up their spouses. While this may work well, we have seen many instances when it generated a classic vicious circle. He resists "being remodeled into the image of some damn university shrink." She tries even harder to "get you in touch with your own feelings." He gets more remote and defensive and she get more and more desperate to "open up" their relationship. His dark fantasy is that if he gets involved in her world of freed-up emotions and therapy buzz words, he will have to change his whole comfortable way of thinking and feeling and acting. Her dark fantasy is that if she cannot get through to him, she will be condemned to a shallow, empty, uptight nonrelationship. Should she be successful in dragging him into therapy, the most profitable issue to deal with is not which lifestyle they should adopt, but how they can disengage from this destructive cycle of pursuit and retreat.

In a previous chapter we considered the negative coalition: the couple who are so reactive to each other that it does not seem possible for one to make a comment without the other making a rejoinder. No work can take place until the therapist helps the couple find a different format for their sessions. Again, the issue is not the content, but the rules of interaction.

The Disengaged Couple

This couple is already emotionally divorced before they come to you. They may be living apart. Perhaps they have already filed for divorce or have at least talked to a lawyer about the possibility. Typically they report that their love has died as a result of hurt or neglect or attrition. It is not uncommon for one or both to have past or even current extramarital involvements. Why have they come to a marriage therapist? Their motivations may vary. For some it is a commitment to the children, or to the joint lifestyle they have enjoyed, or to the idea of marriage "till death do us part." For some the whole idea of divorce is the equivalent of failure and they feel they owe it to themselves to see if the relationship can be revived. For some it may be only a half-hearted gesture to be able to say they left no stone unturned in trying to make it work before they gave up on it completely. Whatever the nature of the motivation, it is never wise to underestimate it. After all, they did care enough to seek out a counselor (which takes more than a little courage) and to commit resources of time and money and self to the enterprise. In view of this it is best to begin with the premise that your contract is to help them have more positive experiences with each other. Some therapists require couples to give up all outside entanglements for the duration of the therapy. Others require that they live together for this period on the grounds that they can't easily enrich their positive experiences with each other if they don't share the same quarters. Perhaps the majority of therapists are more flexible and play it by ear, but in each case the goal is the same.

Early or late it may become evident that no reconciliation is possible because one or both have already completed their disengagement and are just not up to investing again in the marriage. In that case, it is our opinion that the therapist should recommend a reformulation of the therapeutic goal. Without question the most satisfying outcome of therapy for any clinician is to see the marriage reestablished as a living, mutually rewarding relationship. When it becomes very clear that this goal is not attainable, it is of great value to a couple to help them achieve a dignified, humane dissolution. The issue of renegotiating contracts will be treated in the next chapter, as will the style of intervention that has come to be known as "divorce counseling."

Mismatched Commitments: The Enmeshed/Disengaged Combinations

One of the most difficult pair configurations encountered in triangular therapy involves one spouse who is very committed to the marriage and one who is disenchanted and largely uninterested in maintaining the relationship. A variety of motivations may account for the disengaged spouses agreeing (often reluctantly) to come into joint therapy. It may simply be a matter of yielding to pressure from the spouse and others, a means of temporarily placating them. Sometimes it is a matter of guilt or shame, feeling they owe the marriage this one last chance to succeed. Sometimes it appears that the real motivation is to get the spouse into the hands of a good therapist before making the final break; in effect, dumping the abandoned spouse on the therapist's doorstep.

Whatever the underlying mixture of motives, the first task is to determine whether a viable joint goal can be found. With one partner pushing hard for a reconciliation and the other finding it difficult even to get enthusiastic about exploring various alternatives, we find ourselves confronted head on with what Willard Waller (1938) once called the *principle of least interest*. This principle is that in a relationship, the partner who has the least interest in maintaining the relationship controls the terms of it. Under these circumstances the principle is usually easy to observe in operation. The chances are that any real contract for therapy will have to be largely on terms acceptable to the less-enchanted partner. The other is quite likely to go along, even when they object to the arrangement because they perceive themselves as having little choice. To go along is the only chance they see for attempting to save the marriage. Their perceptions may be accurate. Sometimes, however, the disengaged spouse requires so much freedom or such massive capitulation on issues of central importance to their mate that no joint therapeutic contract is possible. In that case, as we shall discuss more fully in the next chapter, joint therapy is not possible and the therapist must choose to work with one or the other in individual therapy or with neither.

ADDITIONAL DIAGNOSTIC CATEGORIES

Mismatched Scripts

Beyond the couple's place on the enmeshed-disengaged continuum, there are other diagnostic issues that cut across the gross "anatomical" categories. We have already alluded to *mismatched scripts* as a common source of difficulty in many marriages. Every person comes to a marriage with an ideal of what he or she has a right to expect in marriage. Typically, it has never occurred to them that any mentally healthy, right-thinking person would not share their views on the subject. Everyone knows that couples go to bed at the same time or that women should do the laundry, or that when you are sick whoever loves you brings you chicken soup, or that decent men don't ever physically abuse their wives, or that men are supposed to initiate sex, or that every evening meal includes green vegetables, or that everyone takes a bath every day and cleans out his or her tub afterward, or that no loyal spouse would ever discuss personal matters with an outsider, especially relatives. Such beliefs are frequently unexamined and primitive. They have been taken for granted for so long that to challenge them is to reveal a basic moral or intellectual or cultural deficiency in the challenger. No couple can avoid running into mismatches in their scripts, but some seem to be especially plagued by this problem, either because there seems to be so many important areas where they see things differently, or because the contested issues are of such central symbolic significance to one or the other of them. The diagnosis suggests that couples need to reframe the problem so that it is not viewed as a question of each other's basic intelligence or character or commitment to the marriage, but merely of different backgrounds and life experiences. Once the differences are understood more sympathetically and divested of some of their emotional and moral charge, it becomes possible to negotiate jointly acceptable scripts in these areas of dispute. Strategies may vary depending on the place of the couple on the enmeshed-disengaged continuum.

Another diagnostic issue that cuts across couples' styles is *communication skills and styles.*

Communication Problems

It is uncommon to see a couple in therapy whose level of communication skill or communication style does not contribute to the problem. The four most frequent issues are: (1) sheer absence of opportunity for meaningful discussion due to over-heavy schedules or competing activities (TV, hobbies, young children, friends, etc.); (2) deficiencies in listening skills and limited ability to express feelings and needs without withdrawal or attack; (3) overrich mix of negative to positive affect in spousal exchanges; (4) incongruence between the content of messages and the style with which they are presented (metamessages); also, habitually competitive or hypercritical or weak metamessages.

Individual Psychological Problems of One Spouse

It may be that one partner is going through an episode of deep depression, or exhibiting symptoms of disorientation, or hypochondria, or manic flights of ideas, or unsupported suspiciousness. It is, of course, a matter of clinical judgment as to whether the treatment of choice ought to be couples therapy in such cases.

Indications that this might be a viable treatment modality include any evidence that the pair conflict contributes significantly to the individual symptoms or that the partner's support would be a crucial element in any effective treatment plan. If the problem seems to predate the relationship and to operate relatively independently of it, referral to a therapist specializing individual approaches is probably indicated.

ALL THE THINGS THAT CAN GO WRONG

In our experience there are a number of things that can go wrong in establishing an effective diagnosis. First of all the therapist may be misled by the couple, or deceived by his or her own prejudices, or just too inexperienced to read the situation accurately. As a result he or she acts on an incorrect premise and the attempts at intervention are ineffective. That is, nothing good happens in the relationship. Worst of all something destructive may happen, but most often everyone just gets stuck and nothing helpful happens. Whenever that occurs the therapist needs to reevaluate and rediagnose. This is very difficult to do alone, but a colleague or supervisor almost always brings a fresh perspective and makes obvious what may be a blind spot for the therapist. Naturally this happens a lot more often among beginners, but no one is immune, and we estimate that even an experienced therapist starts off on the wrong foot with perhaps 5% of his or her cases.

A second mistake is to freeze on a diagnosis that is right on target at the beginning, but becomes increasingly irrelevant as the therapy proceeds. We have sometimes discussed diagnosis as though it were a single decision that is made (and announced) in the first session. Actually it is an ongoing process that may well shift as the couple progresses. We will discuss the constant updating of goals in more detail in the next chapter.

Finally, it must be noted that clients may come in with very firm ideas about what their problem is and how it is to be treated. Sometimes they are so rigid and off-base that one can do nothing but refuse to assume the therapeutic role that they prescribe and let them go elsewhere. But often a skilled therapist can establish enough rapport to successfully confront them with the more germane diagnosis they have been afraid to look at.

We are reminded of a couple who came in one time seeking sex therapy. There was some validity to their self-diagnosis, in that sex figured prominently and negatively in every stage of their relationship. When they met he was a 37-year-old celibate priest and she was a sexually active single parent. She freely acknowledged that she "seduced him out of the priesthood." When they got married he discovered that, although she was experienced in this area, she was never orgasmic. As he "worked on this" she became less and less responsive. Having heard of Masters and Johnson's successful technique for dealing with such problems they referred themselves in and prescribed standard sex therapy for themselves.

It became apparent in the first interview that sex was only one of a galaxy of problems they had. Almost every interaction, including intercourse, was a power struggle for this enmeshed couple. Yet whenever the discussion veered from "the reasons we came in," they balked. Sexual dysfunction was the only diagnosis they would tolerate.

So, after laying some groundwork, the therapist sent them home to begin a series of nondemand pleasuring exercises. They were supposed to spend one hour on the assignment each of four nights that week. But they never got around to it. Their excuses were plausible enough. The bedroom was drafty and she had caught a cold. Relatives had come over and had stayed late. An important report had had to be finished one evening, and so on. But they would do it next week.

The next week, however they did not. The excuse was even better: *Shogun* had been on TV every evening until late and....

Having estimated that sufficient rapport existed to sustain the confrontation, the therapist pushed a rediagnosis.

Therapist: You know, I am beginning to wonder if you really want this sexual problem solved.

Wife: I hate the way you psychologists overinterpret everything. Take our word for it, we want to change or we wouldn't be paying you good money to help us with it. It's just that this last week. . . .

Therapist: Convince me. What do you think it will be like when you have solved the sexual problem?

Wife: Well, for one thing, it would make him very happy. He hates it when I don't feel anything.

Therapist: Does he deserve to be that happy?

Wife: What kind of a crack is that?

Therapist: What wonderful things has he done for you that he deserves having you knock yourself out to make him happy?

Wife: Not a damn thing! Well, never mind him, then. It would make *me* happy. You think I wouldn't like to be a fully sexually functioning woman?

Therapist: I don't know. What is a fully sexually functioning woman like?

Wife (Starting to cry): She's a whore. Well, then, never mind me, never mind him, *we* need it. Our marriage needs it. Good sex would at least be something to bring us closer.

Therapist: Do you want to be closer to this man? Do you want to become more dependent on him? Do you trust him?

Wife: Hell no! I don't trust him any further than I could throw him.

Therapist: I can't figure out why you don't do the exercises.

By this point it had become clear to everyone that the problems they had were far more fundamental than her sexual dysfunction. Sex therapy might well be an eventual step in their work together, but more fundamental issues needed to be addressed first. In this case no real progress could be made until the couple's incomplete and inappropriate diagnosis had been replaced by one that was comprehensive and closer to the reality.

SUMMARY

Diagnosis in triangular therapy needs to focus on the structure and style of the relationship between the two clients. Any set of diagnostic categories needs to be flexible enough to accommodate a wide variety of marital problems. The model developed here focuses on the degree of the bonding in the relationship and on the issue of symmetricality. Also, special isues such as mismatched scripts, ineffective patterns of communication, and individual symptomology need to be considered. Diagnoses can be off target altogether, or overly rigid so that they do not shift as the couple shifts its focus over the course of therapy. In such cases consultation for the therapist is of enormous value. Also, diagnoses can be accurate, but rejected by clients. Building up sufficient rapport is essential before pushing a confrontation on the issue.

We suggested at the beginning of the chapter that a good diagnosis implicitly suggests an appropriate intervention. In the next chaper we will examine goal selection and the triangular contract.

5

Establishing the Triangular
Therapeutic Contract

There is some logic to placing this chapter on contracting after the chapters on rapport-building and diagnosing. The core of the therapeutic contract is the selection of joint goals and the commitment of each party to make every effort to achieve them. This step could scarcely be achieved without first establishing a good working relationship between the therapist and the couple, and putting the problem in some focus with an on-target, motivational diagnosis.

On the other hand, some elements of contracting precede every other aspect of therapy. For example, before the first meeting can even take place there must be agreement among the parties on when and where and usually how long the session will be. Frequently the fee and various aspects of the format of the sessions (such as whether they will be conjoint or separate, whether psychological testing will take place, etc.) are negotiated by phone before the parties ever get together face to face.

In this chapter we do wish to begin by discussing some of the issues involved in setting up these initial contractual understandings, even though they come out of temporal sequence at this point. Then in the body of the chapter we will consider the key sequence of steps that logically grows out of establishing working rapport and an effective diagnosis, which we have labeled *achieving a triangular therapeutic contract.* Among these steps are: (1) agreeing upon *process goals* *goals* (that is, establishing an effective style of interaction in the sessions), (2) negotiating *joint outcome goals* (that is, coming to some consensus among the three parties as to what would be accepted as a successful outcome for the therapy), and (3) committing each party to assume appropriate responsibility in working toward these jointly agreed-upon goals. Also, we will consider the circumstances that might lead the triad to renegotiate their contract in midstream, as it were.

One word about logical and temporal sequences before proceeding. It should be clear that in real cases the stages of the therapeutic process rarely play themselves out in the orderly fashion that we have outlined them. In actuality, the process is often less like a well-choreographed dance, in which each step unfolds in elegant sequence, and more like a game among unruly children, in which the steps chase each other in circles endlessly in and out of every session. Indeed, the therapist should be aware that every therapeutic encounter may require the rebuilding or rebalancing of connections with the couple, rethinking the diagnosis, renegotiating the process and outcome goals, and recommiting the members to them.

SETTING UP THE INITIAL CONTRACT

In setting up the initial contract for entering into a therapeutic relationship, there are several categories of issues that must be addressed, such as what the costs of this experience are likely to be for the couple, what degree of competence, availability, confidentiality, and neutrality are offered by the therapist, and what style of intervention format will be followed in the course of the therapy. Probably most therapists do not explicitly discuss all of these issues with each client, yet each client will form some opinion on each, and more than one therapeutic relationship has run into deep trouble because the parties had quite different ideas of the terms of the initial contract.

Client Costs

The most obvious costs of the therapeutic experience for the client are probably the emotional courage it takes to seek out help in the first place, the fee charged, and the time demanded away from other life responsibilities.

Emotional Courage

It is easy for clinicians to forget that it takes a great deal of personal courage—willingness to risk—to bring one's problems to a third party. Those who mobilize themselves to do so have already distinguished themselves from others who have perhaps worse problems, but insufficient strength to extract help from the community in the form of marital therapy. Many report that this is a last resort for them. It is as though their last resource of hope has been spent in putting themselves in the hands of the therapist. None of us are in a position to promise such couples that we can solve their problems, but we can and should reassure them that they have taken a step in the right direction in coming to us, that we will work hard to help them find solutions to their problems, and that we understand and appreciate the courage it took to come.

Fees

One of the first and most natural questions prospective clients have in contracting a therapist is, "What do you charge?" Both rates and policies for payment vary among therapists. Some work in institutional settings where they have very little input into the fee schedule. Others are free to charge whatever the market and their conscience will allow. It is our observation that beginning therapists have a hard time charging money for "doing good." Most of us are recruited into the field because of idealistic desires to help those in pain. It may seem crass and exploitative to make people pay for such help. Yet, unless the therapist is supported in some other fashion, economic necessity dictates that they must charge enough to recompense their time adequately and to pay for overhead expenses.

Whatever is charged, one must proceed on the premise that it is appropriate for people to pay for this professional service (just as it is appropriate to pay for fixing TVs or automobiles or eyes or hearts). Negotiating the fee and means of payment is an organic part of the therapy. It follows that the same sensitivity and preservation of dignity is required here as in every other phase of therapeutic process.

Length of Time

Many clients also press for some idea of how long the therapy might be expected to last. This may be difficult for the clinician to answer before he or she has had a chance to get very deeply involved in the case, yet it is a legitimate question. Few clients are so well off that they can ignore the issue of what the total cost of this venture is going to be. They may be prepared to handle a few sessions, but quite unprepared to contemplate a long-term commitment.

Therapists with a very structured approach may feel able to contract for a set number of sessions (such as eight or twelve) right from the beginning. At the other extreme are therapists who refuse to give any idea of how long it may take. They may respond to the question with such phrases as, "That depends on what develops and how hard you are willing to work," or "Please remember that you did not develop these problems in a few weeks and it is likely to take a while to resolve them also. Only on television do you get an instant success."

While either approach is defensible, we prefer a middle road. In our own practice we often contract with the couple for a limited number of sessions (such as four) with the assurance that by that time we should all have enough information to estimate whether we were likely to succeed and whether it would be a shorter- or longer-term process. In our opinion have a prearranged time for an evaluation session motivates both the therapist and the couple to get down to work immediately. It also moves all parties to reevaluate the therapeutic contract at that point.

Obligations of the Therapist

Like all contracts, something is required from both sides. What is it that the therapist agrees to provide in return for the investment of hope, money, and time that he or she requires from the client? We have already acknowledged that he or she cannot promise success. What can be promised is some degree of relevant competence, some prearranged level of availability, some guarantee of confidentiality, and a strong commitment to impartiality.

Competence

The clients have the right to expect their therapist to be competent to handle the problems they present. In given cases, quite specific competencies may be required. For example, if a therapist has had little or no training in working with sexual inadequacies or overweight or alcoholism or divorce mediation, it is unethical to accept clients with these needs without commenting on one's lack of experience in these areas. When this sort of situation arises, the ethical therapist will refer the couple to a more experienced colleague or, if one wishes to expand one's experience in these areas, one ought to obtain supervision or ongoing consultation on the case.

Availability

Therapists have different lifestyles and circumstances. Some deal with very disturbed clients and feel that they need to have a 24-hour answering service that can alert them in case of an emergency. Others are quite strict about receiving calls only during office hours. Some are available for early morning or lunch hour or late night emergency sessions on short notice, and some are not. Whatever the case, the clients should understand at the beginning what they are (and are *not*) getting in terms of availability.

Confidentiality

All therapists are bound by the standard conventions of confidentiality. Yet there are many variations even within this ethical standard. For example, interns may need to tape or videotape sessions or have live supervision as part of their training. Often these materials are shared not only with a supervisor but with a group practicum. Clients should understand exactly who will have access to this tape, what eventually will happen to it, and so forth. Many therapists take process notes or keep running case summaries. Clients have a right to know who has access to those files, what sort of information is in them, how their confidentiality is protected, and how long they will be kept.

Also, therapists have different philosophies about keeping the confidences of one spouse from the other. Some feel that permitting any such unshared secrets is subversive to the therapeutic process. Others respect the right of each to privileged communication. In either case, the client should understand explicitly the policy of the therapist. In particular, there may need to be some agreement that neither client will subpoena the record for any future court battle.

Neutrality

One of the most serious doubts new clients have is whether the therapist is going to side with themselves or their spouses. In Chapter 2 we looked at the principle of symmetricality in detail. This is, of course, merely one manifestation of that principle. Commitment to it needs to be convincingly evident from the first session.

Format of the Session

Clients come with a wide variety of ideas about what the therapeutic process will be like. Their expectations (and sometimes fears) may be based on previous experience with therapists, on what they read in books or saw on television, or what friends or relatives have told them, or on their own imagination. It is wise, therefore, to give them at least a general idea of what they may expect right from the beginning. For example, will the sessions all be joint or will they meet separately with the therapist some of the time? Will they be scheduled weekly or every other week or twice a week or on some variable schedule renegotiated each time they come? What will the sessions themselves be like? Will their values and personal style be respected, or will they be pressured to do things that might embarrass or offend them? Will they have reading or other homework assignments? Can this therapist be counted on to give advice and propose solutions, or is this one of those who assiduously avoids expressing any opinion?

The answers to these questions will depend on the therapist's style and on the nature of the couple's problem. In this section we should like to consider briefly some of the issues of therapeutic format. Others will be discussed in the context of particular intervention strategies later in the book.

Conjoint Versus Separate Sessions

It is our prejudice that the problems of couples can best be dealt with in a triangular conjoint session. In a real sense the relationship between husband and wife is the client, and it is not easy to do effective work on that unit when it is not present. Many therapists choose to see each partner separately at least once in the first two or three weeks so as to establish good personal contact with each and observe each operating with and without their partner present. Some feel it imperative to take personal family histories and that the most efficient format for this is one-on-one. Some argue that it is important to give each an opportunity to tell any secrets that he or she doesn't want the spouse to know or at least doesn't want the spouse to know has been revealed to the therapist. Other therapists avoid separate sessions because they wish to avoid being seduced into sharing secrets with one spouse at the expense of the other's trust. Whatever the philosophy, it is crucial to make one's policy of confidentiality clear to each party. Our own policy is to check with the client at the end of a private session and ask, "Is there anything that you have said that you absolutely would not want me to mention to your spouse? Of course, I would in any case try to use good judgment." Sometimes they list some things that they feel would be hurtful and unproductive to communicate. Where we feel that the material could be helpful if introduced appropriately into a joint session, we may try to persuade the client to give us permission to do so. If we do not get such permission, of course we respect the confidence.[1]

---

1. *There are special circumstances in which this confidentiality cannot be assured. For example, most states require that child abuse be reported and also threats of harm to self or others. These important issues need to be understood in the context of the laws of the state in which a person practices. It is not possible to cover them adequately here, but the reader should be sure to become informed on them in order to practice ethically.*

In addition to early data gathering, we have mentioned in earlier chapters a number of reasons for choosing to see the clients separately for one or more sessions:

(1) To establish symmetrical rapport when there is a problem in connecting equally with each partner.
(2) To let one or the other partner "tell the story," sparing their mate from hearing it one more time.
(3) To negotiate a constructive agenda one-on-one, having failed to break up the negative coalition in conjoint sessions.
(4) To support each partner when the commitments of each are irreconcilably different and you can no longer sustain the illusion of working toward joint goals.
(5) To work with individual issues that are not rooted in the marriage per se even though they may have consequences for it; for example: childhood abuse or incest, relations with their own parents, or unresolved issues from a former marriage. In some case individual emotional problems such as depression may also be dealt with in separate sessions, although it is our preference to deal with this type of symptom in joint sessions.

There are, of course, some risks in seeing each partner separately. Among them are:

(1) The risk that one or the other will fear that the partner will utilize the separate session to establish a coalition with the therapist against him or her or at least to bias the therapist.
(2) The potential of separate sessions developing a life of their own such that the focus of the therapy drifts away from pair issues to individual issues without ever really being renegotiated by all of the parties involved.
(3) The temptation to label one partner as the identified patient whose personal problems are at the root of all pair difficulties.

Style of Intervention

It is important for therapists to let clients know in advance if they are likely to be subjected to any particularly confrontive or intensive interventions. In fact, it is our belief that if the therapist intends to use any very dramatic interventions, from body massage to behavioral homework, from hitting each other with batakas to role reversals, from talking to an empty chair to viewing explicit sexual material, it is good practice to explain the purpose and nature of such interventions carefully in advance. Otherwise the clients may find themselves in a situation they had not bargained for.

Even those of us who restrict our practice pretty much to talking may want to explain to the couple at the end of the first hour that this is the general style that they can expect in every session. You hope they find it helpful, but in any case, "what they see is what they get." This helps to dispel any fears or hopes they may have concerning a more dramatic intervention in a future session.

SETTING PROCESS GOALS

Irrespective of the therapist's initial explanation of how the therapy will be conducted, many husbands and wives come into therapy with a clear agenda of their own as to how things need to proceed. The husband, for example, may feel strongly that it is necessary to report every detail of their troubled history. The wife may have a quite different goal for the session, namely to expose him for the unprincipled, insensitive, hypocritical boor that she finds him to be. Or he may come in to have her cured for her neurotic frigidity while her agenda may be to lay their contested views of the marriage before the therapist for an impartial judgement as to who is right. His agenda may be to enlist the help of the therapist in getting her to give up her lover or hers may be to deposit her unstable husband on the therapist's doorstep so that she can leave the marriage with a good conscience.

In these examples the agendas are not only at odds with each other, but each is also promoting a style of interaction that lacks one or more of the qualities that most therapists consider essential for therapeutic work to be accomplished. An effective session provides interaction that is (1) *symmetrical*, giving each partner a chance to express his or her feelings and needs; (2) *safe*, providing an opportunity to express feelings in an atmosphere that reduces the risk of being attacked or punished; (3) *constructive* rather than adversarial or irrelevant; and (4) *focused on the style of interaction* (second level) rather than on the tiresome details of their daily confrontations (first level).

Many sessions flow smoothly along in exactly this hoped-for fashion without much effort on the therapist's part. But where couples bring in destructive agendas, the task of the therapist is to bring the triangular interaction around to the point where therapeutic change has a fair chance of occurring.

ALL THE THINGS THAT CAN GO WRONG

Based on our own clinical practice, we nominate the following types of clients as among those most likely to sabotage the establishment of a working agenda. Some we have already encountered in the "All the Things That Can Go Wrong" sections of previous chapters.

(1) *The Negative Coalition—Complementary Style.* In this couple one is weak, one is strong; one is good, one is bad; one is active, one is passive. In Chapter 2 we discovered some of the problems in establishing symmetrical agendas in these cases. The same therapeutic strategies apply. In this category are two particularly tough "agenda bandits" (if we may coin a term) worthy of special mention:

    (a) *The Total Holdout.* One partner manifests his or her passive control by refusing to say anything. The power struggle is with the therapist as well as with the spouse.

(b) *The Strategic Holdout.* Here the passive member will talk about anything except the pertinent issues. When they are introduced this partner clams up with, "I'm sorry, I just don't feel like talking about that. OK?!"

(2) *The Negative Coalition—Symmetrical Style.* This pair of evenly matched gladiators was discussed in Chapter 3.

(3) *The Usurper* who challenges the therapist directly for control of the session. This type was also discussed in Chapter 3.

(4) *The Co-Therapist* who immediately aligns with the therapist. His or her attitude is that this therapy team must work hard at untangling the sad story of the spouse's neurosis.

(5) *The Story Teller* who feels compelled to give a full and detailed account of some series of events, complete with with full-scale consulations with their spouse on what day of the week it happened, what the exact sequence of remarks was, how each person felt at each point, and so on.

(6) *The Denier* who resists any implication that there is anything *really* wrong with the marriage and insists that everyone is making too much of this (often in the face of a spouse's attempted suicide, filing for divorce, violence, etc.).

(7) *The Grand Exiter* who either stalks out of the room in high dudgeon ("I don't need to sit here and take any more of this!") or flees the room in uncontrollable tears ("I can't stand this, I don't want to live!"), this in each case because of the spouse's expression of a hurtful or uncomplimentary opinion, or breaking a family rule not to talk about a taboo subject.

In some of these cases the great challenge is to establish symmetricality, in others, safety, in others a constructive, rather than a destructive, mode of communication and in others a metalevel rather than a content-level focus. Unless these immediate process goals are achieved, no more ambitious long-range goals are likely to be achieved.

It should be emphasized that, in our opinion, it is not the therapist's responsibility to succeed against all odds. It is his or her responsibility to utilize all of his or her skills and persuasive ability, but clients have a right to choose to fail. In such an instance, however, the appropriate therapeutic response is not indignation or resentment or labeling them with a terminal diagnosis. In our opinion the response that is more appropriate and most likely to be helpful is what we have called Therapeutic Sadness. We will have more to say about this in the next section of the text.

For the most part we have elected to defer a full discussion of treatment strategies until later in the book. It may be useful however to sketch a few techniques for dealing with some of these cases at this point, if only to reassure the reader that even difficult couples can be helped.

For example, let us consider the couple in which one partner chooses to be a Total Hold Out (type 1a). This is a problem of symmetricality and it may yield to some of the strategies we discussed in the chapter on establishing symmetrical rapport. The therapist might assume the role of spokesman and interpreter of the silent partner, estimating his or her feelings from the material given by the participating spouse and from physical cues. Or, he or she may break up the couple for part of the session and interview the silent partner face to face, disengaged from the pair power struggle. Or, taking advantage of the power struggle, the therapist might decide to attempt a paradoxical maneuver. "I admire the strength and courage it takes to come to a therapist and remain silent despite all the pressures to speak. Whatever you do, don't give in. Your integrity is on the line. There are not enough people today who are willing to stand on principle even when it is costly." Or, "I have to hand it to you. You are a very powerful person. I can see that you run this relationship pretty much the way you want it because she (he) is no match for you."

The point of all this, of course, is to get the Hold Out to disengage from the power struggle and enter into a working therapeutic triologue. It is clear, however, that a couple who achieves this short-range goal has also demonstrated their ability to achieve an important long-range goal—learning to negotiate their differences without getting locked in a power struggle.

The Story Teller (type 5) presents a different problem. It may be that no real intervention is possible until he or she has been given the chance to have their story heard. The therapist may choose to listen to it one-on-one. This spares the partner one more rehearsal of a tale he or she has heard a hundred times. It also prevents the symmetry of the joint sessions being sacrificed to the compulsive need to get the whole narrative out. As soon as practicable, however, the focus must be turned from the past (about which nothing can be done) to the present. At some point in the narrative the therapist might ask, "How do you feel right now about the things you are telling me?" Or, if both are present, the question might better be addressed to the other partner (thus introducing symmetry as well as relevance), "How do you feel as your spouse recounts these painful experiences?" Another possible stopper might be, "That is a very unhappy pattern you are describing. How can we find a way to shift from that way of interacting to something that works better for both of you?" If the client's response to this intervention reintroduces a first-level focus, "The only thing that could really help is if he quit spending so much money on his damn hobbies," the therapist's job is to reframe it at a higher level, for example, "To me it seems that the real problem is the different priorities you two have in the marriage" (second level, mismatched scripts).

One more example: the Denier (type 6) can be approached in at least two different ways with some hope of success. The therapist could take him or her at his or her word and proceed on the assumption that there is no serious problem and therefore no serious impediment to making sensible, helpful changes in the relationship. Then the therapist could proceed to recommend changes that the spouse desperately wanted. Either the partner would feel obligated to live up to his or her "can do" image and yield in these crucial points, or, more likely, would agree but then not follow through. In the latter case the therapist can use the failure as documentation of the power struggle at the root of their problem.

Other approaches might be to express to the client relentless sadness that he or she does not even have permission to acknowledge his or her pain. Or, contrariwise, one could rejoice with him or her that he or she is able to stay so calm and unruffled in the face of so many stressful, unresolved issues. Both of these approaches are calculated to subvert the denial. In both cases the denial is denied its function as a defense by being labeled a strong indicator of the pain it attempts to hide. These are paradoxical moves on the part of the therapist, in that the situation is defined so that the harder the Denier tries to hide his or her pain, the more evidence of the intensity of the pain.

To summarize, the immediate goal in triangular therapy is to establish a style of interaction in the sessions that is symmetrical, safe, constructive, and focused on the appropriate level of diagnosis. In some cases this type of interaction occurs spontaneously and effortlessly from the very beginning of therapy. In others the therapist must proceed around the full circle of Parsons's categories, utilizing acceptance, support, intervention, and reinforcement of new behavior just to get the therapeutic triangle operating.

In either case, once an effective style of interaction is established, the three members of the triangle are confronted with the necessity of negotiating joint long-term goals and contracting with each other to work toward them.

ESTABLISHING OUTCOME GOALS

The role of the therapist in helping a couple establish outcome goals is, in our opinion, quite different from his or her role in helping them establish a workable agenda. In the case of process goals, it seems to us altogether ethical and even necessary to utilize every skill, every persuasive means to set up a situation in which work can be achieved. The couple, after all, has come into therapy in hopes that the clinical skills of the therapist would be used in their behalf.

The situation is quite otherwise with longer-term goals. We do not believe that any therapist has the ethical right to impose his or her own life view upon a client. If the couple's religious or philosophical conviction is so incompatible to the therapist's that they cannot, in good conscience, work in honest tandem with them, it is appropriate to refer them to someone who can. This ethical constraint is not always observed by therapists who are heavily committed to a particular life view. It is our strong conviction that this does not make it professionally acceptable. The foundation of the therapist-client relationship is a basic respect for the client's values.

Therapists may, however, play a key role in helping clients clarify their objectives. In those cases where a husband and wife may be headed in different directions it is proper to help them negotiate joint goals. It may also be helpful to redirect their attention to the metalevel rather than the content level. All of this can be done within the bounds of scrupulous respect for the client's values and desires.

Often, when the therapist gets to the core of what each partner wants, it turns out that both want the same thing—a fact obscured by their style of interaction. For example, she may be fighting for more say in family decisions, and he may be fighting for more responsible behavior from her. At the metalevel both may be trying to find a way out of an asymmetrical father-daughter pattern of interaction and into a symmetrical adult-adult interaction. With the issue redefined in this way they can begin relating as teammates, working toward the same ends rather than as adversaries locked in a power struggle. Similarly, a couple rocked by the infidelity of one partner might find that both want to rebuild the marriage if they can be helped past the blame and counter-blame style of interaction they have felt trapped in.

Incompatible, Nonnegotiable Goals

It does occur, however, that a couple may want absolutely, mutually exclusive goals. He wants her to get used to living in the big city where he has a good job. She is absolutely committed to moving back to their rural home state. He wants her to go back to being a traditional wife and mother; she is committed to pursuing schooling or a career. She wants to make the marriage work; he wants to escape from it as gracefully as possible. These are known in the profession as *zero-sum* situations; that is, whatever one wins the other loses, for a net gain of zero to the pair.

In our view there are only three productive strategies available to the therapist when it has become clear that the couple is locked in a zero-sum contest of wills. First, if there is some clue that this issue is really surrogate for a number of other more basic issues, it is often possible to find a solution to the whole system of problems and take the pressure off this one, moving it from "unnegotiable" to "negotiable." For example, in one of the cases alluded to above, the wife simply could not adapt to being in a big city away from her home state and extended kin network. Every summer she took the children and went home for a visit that often lasted for months. He had a highly technical job that he loved and that paid good money, but that required him to work in Los Angeles. There was no future for him at all in the rural area that she felt so attached to and he resented her constant yearning for home, and especially her long vacations. Each partner was absolutely adamant, neither would give an inch. In examining the relationship more deeply, however, the therapist found that the marriage had been a disappointment to the wife from the beginning. He was not an attentive husband, working long hours at his absorbing job. She had been stuck alone for months in a small apartment with first one and then two babies to care for and no real adult network to relieve her boredom and loneliness. It was in this period of their early marriage that the idea of going home became such a fixed idea in her mind, and no wonder. Now that they were more affluent and could afford a nicer home in a better neighborhood, she had no stomach for it and spent all of her emotional energy trying to get him to move back. It became apparent that all of her disappointments in the marriage had become wrapped up in this single symbol. As the couple began to work on communicating with each other more effectively, expressing more affection, making more joint decisions, and utilizing the opportunities that their present community afforded together as a couple, she gradually quit talking so much about her home state. At the end of several months she reported that she could not imagine why she had been so immature about that and said that she guessed she had finally grown up and accepted being married.

In our opinion, if the therapist had insisted from the beginning that the move was not the core issue, this diagnosis would have been rejected by both of them. But by systematically attending to the underlying dissatisfactions, the original issue was gradually put in perspective until it finally became negotiable.

A second strategy is to accept a limited definition of one's therapeutic task, namely, to isolate and clarify (but not necessarily solve) the core conflict. It is often a major project just to disentangle it from all confusing side issues and phony rhetoric. Having clearly identified, isolated, and confronted the irreducible conflict and explored the full range of alternatives, the therapist may define his or her job as largely done. The couple must then decide what to do in the face of this challenge to their unity. For example, in one couple, the wife had a religious conversion experience. Her faith and her involvement in the life of her congregation became the centerpiece of her life. He had been tolerant at first, but came to be resentful and actually hostile toward the church because of the heavy demands it placed on her and because her loyalty to them seemed to far exceed her loyalty to him. After several weeks of therapy they were unable to find any solution to this problem except to live with it. They decided to stay together and the therapist was able to help them to adopt some guidelines to reduce overt conflict, but the underlying issue did not change. Shy of using magic or coercion, no other solution seemed possible.

Finally, the most difficult case of all involves the couple deadlocked over whether to stay married to each other or not. When all of the camouflage is stripped away, the naked truth is that one partner wants desperately to make it work and the other has already emotionally resigned from the marriage. In such cases the clinician may simply have to choose whose therapist to be. If he or she tries to work with both it will inevitably lead to separate sessions since the couple's goals are incompatible. Every session with the committed partner is spent trying to get the therapist to coach him or her in the best tactics for reengaging the outbound spouse. The other partner's sessions are spent working on enlarging and consolidating their gains, now that they have achieved emotional emancipation from the marriage. While each is engaged in legitimate therapeutic endeavor, the therapist, attempting to work with both of them, is put in an irresolvable conflict of interest. We see no ethical alternative but to choose one as the client and refer the other to another therapist.

When the Goal is Divorce

Traditionally, when married persons decided they could no longer tolerate their partners, they sought out a lawyer who helped them select the legal grounds they would use, and directed their efforts to getting everything they possibly could in terms of a financial settlement, custody of the children, and all the rest. Their partners, meanwhile, had to get lawyers of their own. Each called witnesses to testify against the other and it was not uncommon that bank accounts and business records were impounded, furniture removed in midnight raids, injunctions issued—a general legal and emotional donnybrook ensuing. Today most states have made it possible to get a divorce without this type of adversary procedure. In some states the legal steps have been so simplified that a couple may be permitted to file on their own, without an attorney, if they can come to agreement between themselves on the major issues.

Increasingly, couples who wish to avoid an adversarial approach seek marital therapists to assist them in negotiating their disengagement. This type of professional service requires particular skills and a fair amount of special information about the law and the divorce process. It would be easy for a well-intentioned but unknowledgeable clinician to pass on misinformation to a couple in these cases. Even well-informed therapists may be tempted to cross the line between professions and begin giving legal advice (which is unethical and illegal for those not licensed as attorneys). Because of these and other potential pitfalls, *divorce counseling* or *divorce mediation*, as this has come to be called, has developed as a specialized subfield within the profession of marital therapy. Several books have been written on it and extensive workshops are available in many parts of the country. In view of the sensitive interface with the legal system and of the particularly strong feelings associated with the death of a marriage, we recommend that therapists without special training refer these cases to those who have prepared themselves in this specialty.

Sometimes the decision to divorce emerges out of marital therapy as the only solution they can agree upon. Where the couple has already established good rapport and an effective working relationship with one therapist, they may resist being referred to another just because they have redefined their goals. In such cases it is possible to call in a specialist as a consultant to help them with the more technical aspects of the process.

ACHIEVING AN EFFECTIVE CONTRACT: ALL THE THINGS THAT CAN GO WRONG

It is one thing to come to some agreement on goals, it is another to get each partner to do the things they have committed themselves to doing in pursuit of those goals. A number of things can derail the therapy. It may well be that one or the other partner has not been altogether candid in what they really want. They have gone along with their partner and the therapist, but because their own agenda has been stymied they drag their feet or even sabotage the therapeutic program they had reluctantly endorsed.

One example that comes to mind was a couple in which seven years prior to the therapy she had had a brief affair. The issues addressed in the conjoint sessions, however, revolved around current issues; his general passivity, and particularly lack of sexual interest. Each session brought some apparent improvement in communication and mutuality, but between sessions it would all fall apart. Finally, in discussing this process the husband said, "I can't help it, when it comes right down to it my feelings for her are dead."

Counselor: Were they always?

Husband: No.

Counselor: How long have they been dead?

Husband: Years.

Counselor: How many years?

Husband: I don't know. Since her little escapade, I guess.

Wife: That was seven years ago! Don't you believe in the statute of limitations? Give me a break!

Husband: (Silence).

Counselor (Drawing from bits and pieces of data collected in previous sessions): I think I am beginning to see how you feel. Is this right? You feel that she has never, from the beginning, been satisfied with you as a husband. You never finished your education and entered a real profession. You are not the handiman around the house her father was. She has always been disappointed that you did not share your feelings with her or enjoy the plays and concerts that she enjoys. Then seven years ago she found a man who was everything she wanted and even though she came back to you you are afraid to forgive her and let yourself love her again because she really doesn't want you—not the way you are. She wants you to be like that other man. You are afraid to love her for fear of getting hurt. Is that it?

Husband (Silence).

Wife: Is that it?

Husband: I guess you could say so. He hits it pretty close.

Wife: You dummy! I admit I'd like some things different, but do you think I would have come back to you and stayed with you through these seven years of garbage if I didn't love you—even just the way you are I love you more than any other man.

Counselor: Do you believe that?

Husband: I don't know if I do. I'd like to.

This exchange provided the foundation for real therapy to begin. Prior to this point everyone was proceeding as though they had a therapeutic contract, but they did not have one because the husband was not really prepared to participate. The goal of making the marriage work better was threatening to him so long as he felt that his only protection from her dissatisfaction was emotional anesthesia. When the goals of the therapy were renegotiated around this new insight, it was possible to make progress.

In another case, the husband had moved out and taken an apartment before the couple ever came for help. The therapist in this instance joined with the wife in insisting that they could not do real work in the marriage while they were living apart. The husband moved back, but sabotaged the therapy until his resentments about having been forced to move were brought up and dealt with. In our experience, if either partner feels coerced into a contract, it is doomed to fail.

Another cause of failure is the poorly targeted contract; that is, the contract based on an off-center diagnosis. One of our trainees was working with a couple who spent all of their time in an unprofitable exchange of complicated cross complaint. The young therapist was particularly impressed with the irrationality of the husband's outbursts of temper and fits of jealousy. He decided that the man was probably a borderline paranoid schizophrenic and that his best strategy would be to help the wife acquire the strength to leave him. After a few sessions (both joint and separate), the wife contacted the supervisor and registered the following complaint: "I don't think our counselor knows what he is doing. We love each other and he is trying to break us up. He didn't say so, but I can tell."

This brings up still another issue: the covert therapeutic agenda. There is a variety of professional opinion on this point, but it is our strong conviction that it is both ineffective and unethical for the therapist to have a private set of goals for the couple. No matter how much wiser than the couple the therapist may be, he or she does not have the moral right to attempt to impose solutions upon them to which they are not a consenting party.

One final word about the failure of therapeutic contracts. A common error among inexperienced therapists is to accept a contract (explicit or implicit) in which it is understood that it is the role of the therapist to "fix" the couple. That is a foolish contract. The only viable role for the therapist, in our opinion, is to facilitate the couple's taking charge of their own problem and solving it. The therapist is the coach—not the offensive team. In supervising trainees, whenever we see the therapist working harder than the couple we know that the contract will fail.

RENEGOTIATING THE
THERAPEUTIC CONTRACT

Whenever it becomes apparent that the original contract is not working or that the original diagnosis was not on target, it is time to negotiate a new understanding with the couple as to how the therapy must proceed. Sometimes new information comes to light. Sometimes the couple's circumstances change. Whatever the case, it is important to be sure that each partner feels OK about the shift. It is not uncommon for at least one party to feel that the rules are being changed in midstream (as indeed they are). We remember one case in which the original contract was to work on communication and negotiating a set of differences in their lifestyle. Then in one session the wife suddenly said, "This is all foolishness. Why don't we admit to the doctor that the only real problem in our marriage is your drinking problem. If you quit drinking we could handle all the rest of our problems without any outside help." The therapist made the mistake of permitting this change in contract on the spot by saying, "Well, that's probably as good a place to start as any." The husband refused to return. He felt he had been set up. Only months later when he had begun to deal with his drinking in another setting (Alcoholics Anonymous) was he willing to come back into therapy and then only on the terms of the original contract.

SUMMARY

In the last few chapters we have detailed the process of establishing symmetricality, effective rapport, of finding motivational and on-target diagnosis, and, finally, of negotiating process and outcome goals that are designed to resolve the problems the couple came in with. In the next set of chapters we will look at a variety of intervention techniques that may be utilized by the therapist to help the couple in the attainment of these goals.

•

II

Achieving Effective Change

•   •

In Part I we considered some of the issues that must be dealt
with when three people undertake therapy. In Part II we will
consider more systematically the step in Parson's paradigm
that we have called intervention for change, that is, the facet of
therapy that, building upon a foundation of rapport and
diagnosis, attempts to reshape the marital system in some way.
We have noted that different schools of therapy emphasize
different strategies of intervention. Some focus on changing
behavior directly, believing that changes in feelings and
perceptions will follow as the couple acquires new experience.
Others prefer to enter the system in the cognitive realm
following the ancient proverb, "As a man thinketh in his heart,
so is he." These therapists work at helping the couple to
reframe and reconceptualize their relationship, believing that
changed feelings and behavior must surely result. And finally,
still other therapists put their emphasis on the expression and
management of feelings, convinced that once these are

appropriately dealt with, the other two areas will fall into line.

We see no need to decide among these points of view. All are valid. It is not possible to change how a person acts or thinks or feels without changing all three. A competent therapist will be able to intervene at any or all of these points in pursuit of agreed-upon therapeutic goals.

In Chapter 6 we will review the logic and techniques of behaviorally focused intervention. In Chapter 7 we will explore various cognitively oriented strategies, and in Chapter 8 we will survey a range of approaches that concentrate directly on feelings. In Chapter 9 we will complete our consideration of intervention with a discussion of how gains may be stabilized (Parsons's fourth step in the therapeutic process). In that chapter we will also deal with the negotiation of termination and with possible follow-up.

6

Changing Behaviors

Unhappiness in marriage may be viewed as the direct result of destructive or at least ineffective patterns of behavior. Note that our emphasis is on patterns. In our opinion, in this as in other areas, it is crucial to focus on the metalevel and avoid getting bogged down in the isolated details. In order to change behavior the clients and the therapist must identify the patterns causing the greatest difficulty and find alternative patterns of behavior more likely to bring the couple satisfaction.

This chapter will concentrate on behavioral approaches to problems that are particularly disruptive of pair functioning; such things as poor communication, vicious circles, or the inability to negotiate new, mutually rewarding behaviors. We will not deal here with specific behavioral treatment programs, such as those for eliminating phobias and other anxiety states, substance abuse, overeating, and uncontrolled tempers, to name only a few. Such programs may indeed be effective in improving the quality of a marriage, but in our opinion they are best administered individually or in groups rather than in the triangular context.

IMPROVING COUPLE COMMUNICATION

When couples make their own diagnosis of the reasons they don't get along, the most frequently heard is, "We don't communicate." Professionals, too, look to the pattern of communication as the most likely source of difficulty in marriage. After all, communication, by definition, lies at the core of every relationship. In order to be helpful, however, a diagnosis must suggest what it is about the system that needs to be changed. Are important messages distorted or ignored or never sent? Is the prevailing emotional tone of the message critical and negative rather than supportive and positive? Is the couple unskilled in reading and dealing constructively with the relationship-defining component of messages (the so-called *metamessage*) as well as their content? These problems may occur together or separately, but each requires its own behavioral remedy.

Training Couples in Basic Communication Skills

A variety of programs for training couples in communications skills have been developed. They have been described in some detail by their authors (see, for example, Bach & Wyden, 1969; Miller, Nunnally, & Wackman, 1975; Guerney, 1977; Thomas, 1977; Jacobson & Margolin, 1979, ch. 7). We have attempted to abstract a few principles that seem to be crucial from this broad array of approaches. The reader may wish to investigate one or another of these programs in greater depth by going to the original sources.

It is evident that the responsibility for good communication rests equally with the person attempting to communicate a thought or feeling and the person attempting to understand the message clearly. There are specific skills associated with each role. The job of the sender is to frame his message in such a way that it is unambiguous and unthreatening. The job of the receiver is to permit the sender to express the message fully and, before exchanging roles, checking out whether the perceived meaning is congruent with the intended meaning of the sender.

Improving Skills as a Sender

A number of guidelines for more effective sending have emerged out of the various training programs. Among those which we feel are most important are the following:

(1) Accept responsibility for attempting to express your important feelings. Reject the temptation to leave the first move up to your partner or to withhold your feelings.

(2) Assume a posture of trust; that is, exhibit a positive, accepting attitude toward the receiver. The message should be framed *as though* the receiver could be counted upon to be a person of good will, endowed with both the desire and the ability to receive and understand a clear statement. The "as though" is important. It is not necessary to be fully convinced that this is so, only that it is best to behave as though it were so.

(3) Use a modulated, direct tone of voice, avoiding a loud, whining, or insistent tone.

(4) Avoid statements that are directly hostile, attacking, belittling, sarcastic, or threatening. It is, of course, appropriate to express anger or hurt or disagreement, but this should be expressed in a nonthreatening way. For example, "I am still upset about last night. It is hard to feel that you care about me when you seemed to ignore me all evening," rather than, "You don't love me! It was totally insensitive of you to ignore me all evening! You must think I have no pride at all!" and so on.

(5) Own your own feelings and avoid telling the other partner how they feel and think. That is, use "I" messages
rather than "you" messages.
(6) Where appropriate, use direct eye contact and a nonde-
manding touch to establish a reassuring bond while discussing potentially difficult subjects.
(7) Communicate positive as well as negative feelings.
(8) Deal with one issue at a time.

Senders who succeed in incorporating these principles into
their style of communicating will be less likely to confuse or
threaten their partners, and thus be more likely to have their
thoughts and feelings received and understood.

Improving Skills as a Listener

In some ways teaching good listening habits is more
difficult than teaching good sending habits. For one thing,
the motivation is different. Nearly everyone wants to be
understood. There is a great deal of variation in how
committed people are to want to understand others.
Given the motivation, there are only a few rules for being a
good listener:

(1) Bend your whole attention to what the sender is saying,
focusing particularly on the feelings implied or expressed in the content of the message, and also in the
tone, posture, and style of delivery.
(2) Refrain from defensive or controlling responses, such as
interrupting, criticizing, amending, contradicting, or
evaluating the sender's message.
(3) Before replying to the message with your own feelings
on the matter, make sure you understand the feelings
expressed by checking out your understanding with the
sender. There are many ways of doing this ranging
from, "Boy, are you upset. I had no idea how upset you
were over this," to the more traditional "Let me see if I
understand your feelings, you feel strongly that . . . "

ALL THE THINGS THAT CAN GO WRONG

It is not difficult to teach these skills to a couple. With the therapist on hand to model the new technique and to coach the couple in their initial efforts, most couples can master these skills in a few sessions. However, learning to be a good communicator when under the watchful eye of the therapist is not the goal of the intervention. Many can achieve near perfection in these circumstances and yet revert immediately to the most unproductive styles of communicating (such as "stonewalling," attacking, telling the other person how they feel, interrupting criticizing, etc.) the first time an upsetting emotional issue comes up at home.

In order to effect a transfer of learning from the office to the home, it is helpful to give homework assignments. These give the couple experience in dealing with everyday problems using their newly acquired skills between sessions. It is also important to follow the couple over a period of time to help them work through the difficulties they find in shifting from old habits to new ones. Fortunately, communication skills are self-reinforcing when correctly used. Nearly everyone would prefer to exchange expressions of feelings in a safe, constructive mode than in a dangerous and adversarial mode. When couples seem to make little headway in transferring these skills into their private communication systems, one has to assume that there is a reason for it. Some of the most commonly observed are:

(1) Despite success in practice sessions, the couple feel little sense of mastery over these newly acquired skills. When pressure is encountered in the real world, they do not trust themselves to use the skills, falling back instead on habitual responses. The therapeutic response here might well be to invest still more time in training, with the emphasis being on homework.
(2) One (or both) partner(s) may not be committed to the ostensibly joint goals of therapy and signal his or her real position by refusing to use the skills being taught.

This situation calls for a rediagnosis and a renegotiation of goals.

(3) The couple may be locked in a power struggle with each other and/or with the therapist. The refusal to change behavior is only a symptom of the more pervasive diagnosis. In our opinion, behavioral approaches are particularly vulnerable to this sort of sabotage. One might do better with a cognitive intervention that aims at reframing the situation (see Chapter 7).

(4) Some people place a very high value on variety, spontaneity, and freedom of expression. They are very likely to experience any set of structural rules as intolerably constricting. Such clients are not prime candidates for any form of systematic behavioral induction. They are likely to be more responsive to cognitive or affective approaches.

Increasing Positive Exchange

By definition, nothing could be more effective in promoting marital happiness than increasing the incidence of mutually gratifying experiences in the relationship. In a sense, the ultimate goal of nearly all triangular therapy is to increase the frequency of positive experiences in the relationship and decrease the frequency of negative experiences. One of the most successful techniques for getting couples to shift their emphasis in a positive direction is simply to ask them to try it for some limited time period.

It is usually best to begin in the session by asking them to suspend their list of complaints and counter-complaints for a few moments, and tell the therapist some things that they really like and admire about the other—things that they hope would never change. Although some couples will resist this request for all the obvious reasons, a large majority will temporarily set aside their adversarial posture and shift into a positive mode. When pushed to do so he may admit that he thinks she is very beautiful, she may acknowledge that he is a great bed partner, he may give her points for being an outstanding mother, she may admire his integrity, he may find her intelligent and sensible, she may compliment him on his sensitivity with her mother. (The therapist may need to help them avoid disqualifiers such as, "She has a nice figure, except she's about fifteen pounds overweight," or, "He's a great fixit man except he's always too busy to do it.") Whatever the list of positives, it is a rare couple that is unmoved by hearing them. Both focusing attention on a mate's strengths and hearing one's own virtues extolled have the effect of strengthening the bonds between the couple. Also, it sets a positive tone, a constructive context, for the rest of the session.

Of course, the therapeutic goal is to enrich the exchange of positive in the private life of the couple, not just in the therapist's office. One way of doing this is to institute a week of "caring days" (Stuart, 1976). Rather than ask what one likes or admires about one's partner, the therapist gets each to list the things that their partner *does* that they appreciate. These are framed in very concrete behavioral terms and the couple is assigned to double or in any case substantially increase several of these behaviors during the coming week and report back. (Each is to monitor only their own, not their partner's behavior.) When couples take this assignment in good faith and carry it out, the results are often dramatic. It is almost necessary to see the transformation to believe it. Even though the specific problem that brought them to therapy may not be resolved, their frame of mind toward each other has so altered that finding solutions to the problem is greatly facilitated.

ALL THE THINGS THAT CAN GO WRONG

Some couples are so angry or hurt or so committed to their own agenda for the session that they refuse to list their partner's positive qualities. Indeed they may deny that there are any. When this happens, the partner is understandably offended. Our strategy is to shift to a reframing mode of intervention. "I see, you have a rule not to say anything nice about her. You must be a very strong person to resist the pressure I have put on you to break your rule. It seems to be a matter of integrity to you. Tell me more about how you came to adopt this rule." Often the response is, "I don't think it is a *rule* exactly. I just don't see much to admire in her at this point." "If it were not a rule, you could find something. I have just met your wife and I can find several things to admire already. If you have no rule, prove it by saying something positive about her." This focuses the couple's attention on the metastructure of their relationship rather than on their specific list of complaints.

When it comes to homework assignments there are at least two things that can go wrong. First, one or both may forget or refuse to do the assignment. Second, one or both may spend the week monitoring and evaluating their spouse's performance rather than their own. This naturally evokes further resentment and resistance in the spouse. Less frequently, one partner misunderstands exactly what it is that their spouse values and the week is spent in conflict over what the assignment really was supposed to be. This can usually be avoided in the first place if the therapist is skillful in setting up the activities for the week. If it does occur, however, the contract will need to be renegotiated.

If for any reason the assignment backfires seriously, it may be wise simply to move away from the behavioral approach for a time.

Intercepting Vicious Circles of Negative Exchange

Among the most common and most destructive patterns of marital interaction is the vicious circle. This pattern can be identified by the following three characteristics:

(1) It is symmetrical and self-perpetuating; that is, whenever the wife does X the husband responds with Y, and whenever the husband does Y the wife responds with X.

(2) There is 180 degrees of difference between each partner's *intentions* and the actual *consequences* of his or her acts. The wife intends that her actions, X, should reduce the probability of Y, and the husband intends that his response, Y, should reduce the probability of X. Neither takes any responsibility for the causal link between their own behavior and the other's response, although each clearly sees the link between the other's behavior and their own responses. Thus, the harder they try/the worse it gets/the harder they try—an escalating spiral of frustration and resentment.

(3) The spiral is supported by dark fantasies on each side as to what would occur if they changed their response. That is, she believes that if it were not for her regular input of X, his Y would run rampant, while he believes that only his Y response keeps her X in check.

The following examples, extracted from my book *Couples: How to Confront Problems and Maintain Loving Relationships*, illustrate both the dynamics of such circles and the types of behavioral intervention that may be effective in interrupting them.

One couple I saw several years ago typified the pattern. He was self-employed in a competitive business that took up nearly all his time. Although he provided well for his family, his wife became increasingly concerned that their two young sons (ages eleven and nine) were growing up virtually without a father. She made a two-pronged attack. First, she took every opportunity to "try to get through to him," explaining how much the boys needed him, how much she needed him. Second, she developed a series of contingency plans designed to "get the best out of him when he was home." That is, when he walked in the door, he was often presented with tickets to the ball game or the circus or the planetarium "for him and the boys." She noted, though, with mounting concern, that despite her efforts he seemed to spend less and less time at home. So she stepped up the program and finally, as part of her increasingly frantic efforts "to get through to him," dragged him in to see me. It took only a few moments to recognize a full-blown vicious circle.

The more she tried to get him to stay home and be involved with the boys, the less he was there. The less he stayed home, the more she contrived. In a private session, he admitted that he was appalled at how miserable his marriage was becoming. He could never relax at home, and although he told his wife that the business was going through a particularly demanding period, he confessed to me that some evenings he stayed at the office and had nothing to do (his office was fitted out with a couch, television set, and bar). In fact, the real reason he had agreed to come to see me was that he had about had it, and if something didn't change he wanted out of the marriage.

The dark fantasy in his case was that if he did come home more, it would just mean more PTAs, baseball games, and nagging. (*Wife*: I don't nag you; I'm just trying to get you to understand how important it is for the boys to have a father). Her dark fantasy was that if she quit nagging him, he wouldn't come home at all. As she put it, "He's hardly ever home now, even with all the encouragement I give him."

Both of them, therefore, were afraid to change for fear things would get worse, and so each kept on doing the very things that were making the situation deteriorate. It was only with the greatest difficulty that I was able to get either of them to budge out of the pattern. I tackled her—alone—first. Here is a fragment of a conversation that went on for about fifteen minutes in the same vein:

C.B.: If I can get your husband to come home by six p.m. three nights a week, can I count on you to let him do anything he wants, even if it's just to watch television? Will you promise not even to make a suggestion as to the program?

Wife: No! What good is he to the boys—or me either, for that matter—if he's just sitting there swilling down beer and watching T.V.?

C. B.: One thing at a time. Let's get him home first. We can try broadening his activities later. This is only a first step. If I can't count on you to cooperate, I don't see how either of us can hope to get your husband to.

Wife: I want to be cooperative, but can't you see the solution is to make him understand . . . ?

Eventually, I got her to say she would trust me for a couple of weeks to see what happened. Then I had to tackle him.

C. B.: If I could guarantee that you would be left entirely alone to do anything you pleased, could you arrange to be home at least three nights a week?

Husband: Hey, I'm in a tough business. There are things I really have to do every night this week. It's not like I was in a nine-to-five job where I let somebody else do the worrying.

C. B.: What would you do if a big deal popped up on the Coast this week and you needed to be there to put in a bid?

Husband: I'd be there. That's the way I do business.

C. B.: So you can arrange your schedule if it's really important to you. Good. I think this may be important. I agree with you that the way things are going, your marriage is in real trouble. In my opinion, if you can shake free about three nights a week, there is a good chance of turning things around. Why not try it for a week or two? I've got your wife to agree to let you spend your nights home any way you want.

Husband: Hey, she could no more quit nagging than quit breathing.

C. B.: Try it.

Husband: One week. But if she starts in on me, that's it.

That agreement took some careful monitoring and nurturing, but within a few weeks the man was spontaneously broadening his activities to include his boys, although he enjoyed wrestling with them or throwing a ball around better than organized outings of any kind.

Whatever the content of the vicious circle, the dynamics

of it are basically the same. I remember an insurance salesman who brought in his "neurotically frigid" wife to be "fixed." His diagnosis was that his wife had been taught by her mother that all men were beasts who were interested only in sex, and that this had so turned her off that even his most enlightened and persistent efforts to turn her on had failed. And he had tried everything. He had read every popular book on sex and several quite scientific ones. He could discuss *The Sensuous Woman,* the *Kama Sutra,* and Masters and Johnson with equal familiarity. He had put up sexually explicit posters in their bedroom; he had taken her to the best, and the worst, X-rated movies; and he had tried every technique known. Nothing worked. At best, he could expect sex about once a month "when she finally gets around to feeling guilty," and even then it was "nothing to write home about . . . she just lies there."

She, it became clear, had not come in to be "fixed." She had come in to expose her husband for the sex-obsessed animal that he was, to let somebody know what she had to put up with. She said, "He's after me all the time. He never walks into a room where I am without grabbing me. Doctor," she said, "when I hear his step on the front porch every sphincter in my body tightens."

Both agreed that it had not always been that way.

Wife: For the first four years of our marriage it was beautiful. What he said about my mother was true. She did warn me about men. So I was careful in my dating. Doctor, the ironic thing is that one of the important reasons I married him was because he was such a gentleman before we were married. I remember congratulating myself that everyone wasn't the way my mother said—that there were a few fine, sensitive men and that I had found one. And you were that way too, at first . . . (cries).
C. B.: Then what happened?
Wife: One night—it was August seventeenth—
Husband: Can you believe this? She has the date memorized.
Wife: I wish I could forget it. Anyway, he came home late that night stinking drunk and wanted to make love. I had never

turned him down before, but he was so obnoxious, and I hate it when he gets like that, so I told him I didn't want to. He said he didn't care what I wanted and tried to force himself on me. There I was in my own bed fighting off a drunken rapist. It was the worst experience of my life. But then to cap it all, the next morning he came in to where I was sleeping in the baby's room, all tearful and hung over and apologetic. Said he couldn't believe he had been so crude. Would I ever forgive him? It wasn't him, it was the alcohol, and so on and so forth. I was beginning to feel that maybe I hadn't been entirely fair, and I was letting him hold me when he started to handle me sexually. I couldn't believe it! After all we had been through!

Husband: Honey, I was just trying to see if you still loved me—can't you understand that?

Wife: Well, it was then that it finally dawned on me what a first-class fool I'd been all this time. I'd been taken in by his sales pitch, just like one of his customers. But the thing is, I had finally learned the truth underneath the sales pitch. It wasn't me he loved, it was sex. He didn't care if it was me or a hole in the mattress, just so he got his precious sex.

Husband: How can you say that? That's a bunch of crap and you know it!

Wife: Well, that's how you made me feel. That's how I still feel. All the pictures and the filth. What has that got to do with me?

Husband: Everything! It's all for you.

Again, the diagnosis is clear. The harder he tries to turn her on, the more resistant she becomes; and the more resistant she becomes, the harder he tries to turn her on. When I saw them, this circle had been getting more and more vicious for almost eight years.

Of course, each one saw half of the circle very clearly: the half for which the other was responsible. He saw that if she were "normal"—that is, sexually responsive—he would not have any need to indulge in his single-minded pursuit of seduction. She saw that if he were patient and gentle she could be as responsive as she had been before the circle began. Each viewed his own behavior as a perfectly reasonable response to a difficult situation, and the other's behavior as inexplicable and sick.

In this case, moreover, it was difficult to negotiate a new pattern. The dark fantasies of both were particularly compelling. In private sessions, each one almost walked out on me when I suggested that changes in his or her own behavior were crucial to the solution.

C. B.: Frankly, Mr. J., I think you ought to just cool it for a while.
Husband: Cool it?
C.B.: Right. Leave her alone. Let her make the advances if she wants to.
Husband: (long silence): Doc, I don't thing you understand my wife. She's just like the business. It takes twenty calls to make one sale.
C. B.: I know that's the way to sell insurance. If you get into a slump, just get on the phone, stop people on the street, hustle until you start to sell again. But your wife simply isn't responding to that. It would pay you just to cool it—do nothing.
Husband (angrily): I'll tell you what I think. I think it's pretty cheap for you to sit there behind your prissy desk and tell me to cool it when you're probably getting it every night and I'm only getting it once a month!
C.B.: Mr. J., how long since you last had sex with your wife?
Husband: Two weeks.
C. B.: Then you have nothing to lose for two weeks. Try it my way for two weeks and if you don't like the way it's going, do whatever you think will work better.

Next, I saw Mrs. J. alone. After attempting to establish some rapport and letting her know that I appreciated some of her feelings, I explained the nature of the vicious circle they seemed to be trapped in. Then . . .

C. B.: It seems to me, that if you wanted to, you could guarantee a break in this circle even if he did nothing to initiate a change.
Wife: (coolly): I'm not sure I get your meaning.
C.B.: Well, if you became the sexual aggressor not only would it shock and please him, but it would certainly put an end to his constant efforts to seduce you.
Wife: Is that your solution, then? Just hop right into bed? (rising, as if to go) I should have known that if we came to a male counselor, that would be his advice!

C. B. (firmly): Mrs. J., please sit down. I have, with great difficulty, convinced your husband that he should cool it for the
next two weeks and leave any sexual advances to you. If he
does so . . .
Wife: That'll be the day.
C. B.: . . . and you make no effort to initiate sexual activity during that period, than I must assume that you prefer it the way
it is and deserve what you get.

I saw them again at the end of the first week. They both
agreed that he had kept his end of the bargain but she had
made no moves. "I will when I feel like it," she said. He
said nothing, but looked at me with a grim smile.

The next week, however, she surprised both him and me
by initiating sex three times. The couple seemed to be
rediscovering all the reasons they had married each other
in the first place. Areas that were not remotely related to
sex began to open up [Broderick, 1979a, pp. 90-99].

NEGOTIATING BEHAVIORAL CHANGES

In the previous sections the changes in the couple's behavior
were instigated by the therapist. Based on the diagnosis a set
of behavioral changes were recommended or assigned that
were calculated to break up unsatisfying patterns of
interaction and enrich the use of positives in the marriage.
Another approach to behavioral change is to supervise the
couple's negotiation of an exchange of behavior so that each
gets something they value in return for doing something which
their partner values. This has been called the quid pro quo
(something for something) approach. In our experiences it is
most likely to succeed when the couple is either playful and
enjoys the game-like aspects of it, or grimly mistrustful and
therefore appreciates the formal contractual features and the
availability of fair-minded third-party arbitration.

Again, to illustrate how this technique might work we quote
from Broderick (1979a, pp. 84-90).

Often, small changes in our behavior—changes that
actually cost us very little—can mean a great deal to our

partner. The first step is for each partner to make a behavioral "wish list"—a list of wished-for changes in his spouse's actions that would make the most difference to him. The second step is to negotiate exchanges from the two lists. For example: I agree to spend at least twenty minutes a day with the children this week (high on your list), if you agree to be more firm in enforcing the television rules we have both agreed to (high on my list).

Instructions for "Negotiating New Behaviors" Exercise

(1) Each partner should give thought to what changes in the other's behavior would make the greatest difference to him. These changes should then be converted into a series of specific goals which the spouse might actually accomplish in a seven-day period. For example, a wife may have felt for some time that the greatest thing her husband could do would be to find a job that had more civilized hours or that didn't call for so much travel. It's not likely that he could actually change his employment in one week, but it is entirely possible (should he agree to it) to send out resumes, follow up leads, or seek interviews within the seven day period.

(2) Next, each should write down three or four of the most desired changes in a "Wish List." To increase the chances for success, the items on the list should have the following qualies:

  (a) Each wish should refer to something the spouse *does*, not something the the spouse *is*. For example, "I wish you would cut down on between meal snacks"— not "I wish you weren't so fat."

  (b) Each item should be specific and concrete rather than vague or general. For example, a wife might say, "I wish you would spend at least fifteen minutes a day talking with me without me having to compete with the newspaper or television"—not "I wish you would talk with me sometimes"; or worse, "I wish we could communicate better."

  (c) Each item should involve behavior that will be observable, so that there is never any question as to whether change has occurred or not. "I wish you wouldn't use that

kind of language in my presence"—not "I wish you
would quit swearing."

(3) After finishing the list, review it to make sure that the items
follow these rules. Also check to see that they are feasible
within the next seven days (there is no sense in a wife's list-
ing the wish that her husband would get home in time for
dinner at least five days next week if she knows he is going
on a three-day trip).

(4) Then share your lists with each other. Be sure you understand every item on your spouse's list—to your spouse's
satisfaction. At this point you haven't agreed to do anything,
so you can afford to push for clarification without commenting on how reasonable, or even how feasible, each item
seems to you.

(5) When both are satisfied that they understand each other's
list, either may open negotiations by making an offer. The
partner may accept or reject the offer or make a counter-
offer.

By way of illustration, I give you the wish lists of one
particular couple, together with the dialogue that
occurred as they negotiated certain key aspects of their
marital scripts:

His Wish List	*Her Wish List*
I wish you'd take better care of the house.	I wish you'd spend more time with the family—at least three evenings a week and weekends.
I wish you'd quit yelling at Rosemarie (the three-year-old).	
I wish you'd be more affectionate in bed.	I wish you'd share your feelings more.
I wish you'd quit smoking.	When I'm not feeling well, I wish you'd help out without my having to ask you.
	I wish you'd pick up after yourself.

Wife: But Mike, I'm not feeling well. You know I never let the
house go to pot when I'm not pregnant.
Husband: The idea is to make a wish list. That's what I wish.
You don't have to do any of it.

Wife: All right, but if you could ever stay home and help me, I'd feel a whole lot more like doing it.

Husband: So make me an offer I can't refuse.

Wife: If you will stay home weekends—

Husband: This is just for a week.

Wife: If you will stay home this weekend and help me get caught up, I will promise to keep the place up for the rest of the week.

Husband: No dishes left overnight in the sink? No clothes dropped all over the living room?

Wife: I'll pick up after myself and Rosemarie, but half the stuff lying around is yours. I don't see why you can't pick that up yourself. . . . Wait, let me write this down. This seems like a fair exchange to me:

(1) I will work with you this weekend to really get this place in shape, and

(2) I will see to it that my things and Rosemarie's are picked up, and

(3) I will do the dinner dishes before I go to bed (this does not mean I have to do any dishes you dirty after dinner) if you will:

    (1) Spend the weekend helping me.

    (2) Pick up your own things.

    (3) Give me a hand in the evenings when I'm not feeling well.

Husband: Okay. It's a deal. Now let's go on to the second item.

Wife: Are you kidding? I'll be lucky if I get all that done this week.

Husband: I'm doing three things on your list and you've only agreed to do one on mine.

Wife: But the things on your list are all huge. I think one is all I feel up to for this week.

Husband: Okay, but let's talk next week about smoking. I don't think it's healthy for the baby.

Some couples find it helps to negotiate penalties to protect a bargain. In the following week, for example, the couple above made a bargain that she would try to show their three-year-old more positives if he would support her efforts at discipline instead of taking the child's side.

Rather than make it an all-or-nothing proposition, they agreed to a penalty if one of them forgot and slipped. He agreed that if he failed to support her, he had to clean the toilet (a job she said nauseated her when she was pregnant). She agreed that if she yelled at the little girl in his hearing, she had to bake him a pie (which she used to do at least once a week before she got pregnant).

Such penalties, obviously, must be agreed to by both sides and should be minor, even fun, concessions. They should be enough trouble to provide added motivation, but not so great a burden as to spoil an otherwise successful week. In a few families, even fines can be effective penalties.

Here's another example from a different couple:

His Wish List	*Her Wish List*
I wish you would quit criticizing everything I do.	I wish you would not ask me to lie for you.
I wish you would not take our troubles to your friend Margaret, and that you'd spend less time with her.	I wish you treated my work with as much respect as you want me to give yours.
I wish you were kinder to my parents.	I wish you would invite some of your friends to the house. We never entertain anymore.
	I wish you would not stay up and read in bed after I'm ready for sleep.

Husband: I really have only one wish: I wish you'd quit criticizing everything I do. The other two are just padding.

Wife: Maybe if you'd do some of the things on my list I'd have less to criticize.

Husband: If you could guarantee I wouldn't hear anything critical out of you for one whole week, I'd do your whole damned list.

Wife: You'd show more respect for my job? I don't think you'd know how. (C. B.: Actually, that's too vague to be easy to comply with.)

Husband: Try me.

Wife: I don't feel good about that. I'll tell you what. I'll do your whole list if you'll do mine.

Wife: I'll only call her twice this week—when you're gone—and I promise not to discuss us—that is our marriage—at all. And I'll phone your mother, although it's not all my fault that she and I don't get along, as you very well know.

Husband: Okay, And I won't ask you to cover for me. Really, though, how often do I ask you to do that?

Wife: All the time.

Husband: Bull! And I will respect the hell out of your job.

Wife: I'm serious!

Husband: *I'm* serious! And I will invite Ken and Edith over for cards. Let's see . . . and I will *not* stay up and read past your bedtime. And you will not criticize me at all, in any way, shape or form, for seven consecutive days. Deal?

Wife: Deal.

Husband: You'll never make it.

This couple did make it, though.

We have sometimes found it useful to use the following form as a guide for this exercise.

Husband's Wish List	*Wife's Wish List*
(1) I wish you would . . .	(1) I wish you would . . .
(2) I wish you would . . .	(2) I wish you would . . .
(3) I wish you would . . .	(3) I wish you would . . .
(4) I wish you would . . .	(4) I wish you would . . .

Negotiated Agreement, Week of _____

Husband Agrees To:

Wife Agrees To:

Negotiated Penalties (Optional):

If Husband Slips, He Agrees To:

If Wife Slips, She Agrees To:

ALL THE THINGS THAT CAN GO WRONG

As in the "caring days" exercise the worst thing that can go wrong is that the couple won't do what they contracted to do. In addition to the possible reasons listed there, we may add another. One partner may decide that in fact, the thing he or she bargained to do is too hard or on the other hand, that the thing they bargained for isn't satisfying when they get it. In either case, the exercise provides valuable agenda for the next session. In fact, a general benefit of well chosen behavioral assignments is that if they work they are effective in improving the relationship and if they do not they still provide valuable diagnostic data.

SUMMARY

When the diagnosis is poor communication or the inability to negotiate joint scripts, therapists frequently turn to behavioral interventions as the most helpful therapeutic response. They may teach the couple communication skills, help them increase the positive exchanges in their relationship, choreograph their disengagement from a destructive vicious circle, or preside over the negotiation of a formal contract for reciprocal changes in their behavior toward each other.

As a general rule such approaches are successful in achieving their aims. At several points we have suggested that where they are not successful, the therapist ought to consider a more cognitively focused approach which involves each person reconceptualizing the relationship and their own part in it. In the next chapter we consider some of the more widely used techniques for helping a couple to change their perspective.

7

Changing Perspectives

As we have seen, behavioral strategies of intervention are based on the premise that marital satisfaction is increased when positive interactions are increased. Cognitive strategies of intervention are based on the equally irrefutable premise that satisfaction is a point of view. After all, what a partner does may be less important than how the act is interpreted in predicting a response. A changed view of the situation is as likely to lead to changed behavior as the other way around.

The most direct approach to this issue may be called *reframing*. Reframing seeks to change the meanings that clients attach to certain stressful patterns in their marital relationship. The object is to find interpretations that lead to a more constructive approach to their problems. For example, before real work can begin it is often necessary to help a couple redefine their "hopeless" problem as "solvable," and their involuntary predicament as voluntary. It is important that they redefine their partner as cosufferer and coworker rather than as antagonist. In revising their diagnosis of their relationship sometimes they need to turn their view of things completely upside down. Perhaps what they viewed as a strength is more usefully seen as a weakness, or perhaps a designated weakness may more realistically be viewed as a resource for survival or an instrumentality of control. They may come to reevaluate behavior formerly labeled loving as actually destructive, while behavior labeled as bad may need to be reinterpreted as showing love.

Cognitive intervention may also be called into service when couples reveal themselves as having quite opposite ways of looking at the world and entirely disparate expectations and rules for marital interaction. In this case the task is *rescripting*, that is, helping the couple to achieve joint scripts and shared perspectives. In the remainder of the chapter we shall look first at interventions that may be classified as reframing and then at interventions that are aimed at rescripting.

REFRAMING

Every therapist develops his or her own favorite techniques for helping clients view their situation with a new eye. Among the most widely utilized are the *rational-emotive* approach pioneered by Albert Ellis and his associates, the *dramatic imagery* approach that, in various versions, is an element in many schools of therapy, and the *paradoxical* approach, associated with Milton Erickson and those he influenced such as Don Jackson, Jay Haley, and Salvador Minuchin.

The Rational-Emotive Approach

Just as there are books written about behavioral approaches, so there are books that spell out the rational-emotive approach in great detail (e.g., Ellis, 1971). For our purposes it is enough to note that it deals with the "tapes" we play in our minds when anything frustrating or upsetting occurs. The object of the therapy is to replace irrational, anxiety-, or anger-generating tapes with rational, level-headed tapes.

Even the imagery of a tape running through one's mind is useful since everyone knows that tapes can be revised or replaced. The issue usually comes up when one partner complains that the other "takes everything wrong," or "is the world's greatest worrier," or "gets upset over nothing all the time." Whenever there is a choice of interpretation in a situation, this person always chooses the most upsetting one and builds it up in his mind until he or she may be almost overloaded by feelings of anger or anxiety.

For example, suppose a man's wife was 45 minutes late in coming home from work. At best this is inconvenient ("Dinner is getting cold," etc.) and worrisome ("I wonder what could have held her up"). Yet many men could parlay such an incident into a major marital crisis through the sheer power of negative thinking. Here are three different examples of what Ellis calls "horribilizing."

Tape of Husband #1: Why isn't she here? Why is it I always end up waiting for her? She could at least call ... but no ... she doesn't even consider me sitting here unable to make any plans until I know what she's doing. If she weren't so wrapped up in herself this wouldn't be happening. I'm not important to her. I really don't think she cares anything about me, despite what she says or she wouldn't be so inconsiderate (etc., etc.).

Tape of Husband #2: She's late. I know she sometimes has to work late but never this late. I don't like her staying after with that creep she works for. I think he has a thing for her. Damn it, where is she? I'll bet they're cosied up in some coffee shop playing footsie. I wonder how long this has been going on? Forty-five minutes overdue. That's long enough for a lot more than footsie. I suppose she'll come waltzing in with some cock-and-bull story about a late report and expect me to believe it, while all this time she's been making it with her boss and I've been too stupid to see it.

Tape of Husband #3: It's not like her to be this late and not call. I'm sure something terrible has happened. She works in a bad part of town. Rape and assault happen there every day. Or it could be an automobile accident. Maybe I should call the hospitals to see if she has been admitted. No, the police ... they'd probably know what's happened to her.

The rational-emotive therapist helps the horribilizing clients to replace such tapes with more rational and less upsetting ones. Any of these husbands could learn to recognize the irrational elements in his own tape and substitute something more reasonable, such as:

I wonder why she's late. Well, no sense worrying about it. She can take care of herself and if she needs any help she'll call. May as well get busy and see if I can get something done while I'm waiting.

This work may be done in private sessions between the therapist and the horribilizer, or in triangular sessions involving the spouse. In either case it is helpful to give the person with the worrisome tapes the assignment to stop and write the tape down verbatim the next time they find themselves horribilizing. When the same situation arises with some frequency it may even be useful to write out a substitute tape and rehearse the new response.

Our own preference is to include the spouse in the session. The insight provided by getting a clearer understanding of what goes on in the spouse's head at such times is often helpful. In addition, partners may be helpful in working out a reasonable and convincing substitute tape. Finally, and perhaps most importantly, they may assume a partnership role in solving the problem by learning to avoid the most provacative triggers to the spouse's horribilizing. This assistance often makes a key contribution in achieving success.

Dramatic Imagery

Imagery and metaphors are very useful devices in helping clients to gain a new perspective on their situation. In the previous section the therapeutic task was cast in the image of changing or editing a tape cassette. By implication the client was led to view this reframing as a straightforward, voluntary procedure similar to one that he had quite possibly performed successfully many times with an actual tape recorder.

In general the use of imagery is most effective when it calls attention to some important but easily overlooked quality of the problem or its solution (for example, that it is hurtful, that it is voluntary, that it is part of a game, that it is expensive, or that it is ridiculous). The connection between the image and the reality it represents must be evident and even compelling if this approach is to have impact, and it is helpful if the imagery is vivid and dramatic.

In the last chapter we cited two cases in which vicious circles were disrupted through behavioral interventions. Here is a case from the same source in which the circle was destroyed by the utilization of dramatic imagery. In this case, as in many others, the key images seem to have discovered the therapist rather than the other way around.

A young couple had been married for five or six years. She had a long list of grievances against him, at the top of which was his getting her pregnant before they were married. Currently, she complained, he was interested in his souped-up car and motorcycle, on which he spent almost all his spare hours. He had no time for her, or the children, or their home. In one incident, he had agreed to put up a new acoustical ceiling in the kitchen, but had left the job half done for six months. In another incident, he had taken everything out of the hall closet to install shelves and then had left the mess in the hallway for weeks. But worse of all, he was becoming increasingly impotent in bed. She felt humiliated and outraged that she was cast in the role of sexual supplicant, especially since he seemed to turn on to girlie magazines and even bra ads in the newspaper more than to her. One night after he had turned her down sexually she woke up and caught him masturbating in the bathroom. "Even the toilet turns you on more than me!" she raged. I must add that she was one of the most acidly critical women I've ever known. Almost everything she said to him was a put-down.

The first few sessions went badly from my point of view. On her part, they consisted mainly of long tirades about what an inadequate husband and father he was, interspersed with tears over her own inadequacies as a wife and mother. He said almost nothing, even vhen I addressed him directly.

C.B.: Well, Mr. S., what is your side of this?
Husband: (Silence, eyes on shoes).
Wife: Well, don't just sit there like a lump of dough, answer the man! We're suppose to be here to get help!
Husband: (Silence).

Finally I said, "Is this how it feels to you, Mr. S.: You just don't feel like performing sexually at night when she's been a castrating wife all day?"

Wife (interest perking up): A what?
C. B. (cursing myself for introducing unnecessary psychological jargon): What I mean to say is, if you criticize him all day, maybe that's—
Wife: What was that word you used?
C. B.: Look, I don't want to get hung up on the word. The idea I'm trying to get across is—
Wife: No, what was the word?
C. B.: (Sigh): Well ... at the turn of the century, in Vienna, there was this doctor named Freud who—
Wife: The word; I want to know the word!
C. B.: Okay, Okay. The work was "castrating." It means—
Wife (slapping her leg and breaking out into convulsions of laughter): I know what it means!
Husband (struggles against laughter and finally gives in).

To me, "castration" was literally a psychological technicality. I knew, of course, what it referred to physically; but in my world, the only time the word was ever used was in the psychological context. She, however, had been raised on an Iowa hog farm where she had helped her father castrate pigs. To her the phrase "castrating wife" called up the outrageously, deliciously vivid image of emasculating her husband with the kitchen shears.

Between gasps, she let me know that she thought it was by far the best suggestion I had made. The session dissolved in tears of laughter. The payoff came later that week, when she opened up on her husband over something and he said to her, "Well, there you go again" and made the sign and sound of scissors cutting. Both of them doubled over in laughter. By the end of the week she had effectively stopped her habit of constant criticism.

As sometimes happens in long-established vicious circles, however, his half of it continued out of sheer momentum for a period of time. At first they both had trouble understanding the concept of passive-aggressive behavior. They had grown up thinking that passive was the opposite of aggressive. Nevertheless, when it finally became clear that forgetting, postponing, neglecting, or withholding could express anger just as effectively as hitting or criticizing, the effect was dramatic. She said, "You mean that when I tell him I need loving, and he tells me, 'Well you can diddle me if you want, but I don't know if it'll do any good,' he's really 'giving it to me?'" (This last phrase accompanied by a strong, obscene gesture). I said, "That's the way it looks to me." That week, when the situation arose, she suddenly sat bolt upright in bed and said to him, "There you go 'giving it to me' again." He got in touch with his anger and had an erection.
[Broderick, 1979a, pp. 99-102.]

Of course, this couple's problems were not fully resolved through the use of these vivid images, but without question, the imagery stimulated a dramatic turning point in their therapy.

Paradoxicals

The use of paradoxical statements to stimulate changed perceptions and behaviors is an integral part of many Eastern religions and has a place also in Christian teachings (e.g., He who would save his life must lose it). In contemporary therapy the idea was most fully developed by Milton Erikson (Haley, 1973), but it has been used in various forms by many therapists.

In its classic form the paradoxical intervention takes the form of attacking a symptom by prescribing it. For example, in the treatment of sexual impotence one assignment sometimes given in the later stages of the therapy (after a few successful erections have occurred) is to give the following homework assignment. "This week during the pleasuring sessions I want Mary to do everything within her power to arouse John, but John, your assignment is to avoid getting an erection at whatever cost. Think about nonsexual things, hum hymns, anything that works. But the important thing is to go the whole week without any erections at all. This is an important step in gaining control of your erections, so I want you to really work at it no matter how provocative she gets. Mary, your job is to make it as tough for him as you can."

There are several things to be said for such an assignment. First of all it puts the couple in a no-lose situation. If he succeeds in avoiding an erection (which seldom happens, incidentally) this is interpreted as having achieved full voluntary control over his responses. "Last week you got erections, this week you avoided them, you have become the master of your own erections." In the more likely event that Mary wins the contest they are liable to face the disappointment with some equanimity in view of the larger goals they came with.

It is important at this point not to take prideful credit for having cleverly tricked them into healthy sexual functioning. Haley says that the best response is simply to appear puzzled, commenting that you can't figure out how they got out of their problem so quickly when the therapy was several weeks from its end. We prefer a somewhat lighter approach. With a twinkle in the eye we are likely to ruefully admit that the world is unjust and the joke is on us. "It just doesn't seem fair that our scientific, sophisticated step-by-step program could be so effectively short-circuited and out-performed by a simple Old-Fashioned American Seduction. Oh well, you can't win 'em all."

As with every other approach we discuss, the magic is not in the technique itself but in the diagnostic judgment that this is the most appropriate intervention with this couple at this point in their therapy. One of the indicators that a couple may be responsive to this sort of intervention is their competitiveness with each other and with the therapist. The more resistant the client, the more effective the paradoxical.

On one occasion a passive-aggressive wife was locked in a power struggle with her husband over the fact that she was a poor housekeeper. He complained that the place was filthy and she accused him of not appreciating how much she had to do, of exaggerating the situation, and so forth. In this case it seemed to make sense to prescribe the symptom. She was told that she was a real person and that she shouldn't lift a finger to do any housework at all that week so that he would know she was in charge of her own life. As his assignment he was encouraged to spend twenty minutes after coming home each day expressing to her his dissatisfaction and frustration about the filthy house. It was explained that this was crucial to his mental health even though it would likely have no effect upon her.

After about five days he gave up on the criticism, rebelling against the assignment, and on the sixth day she followed suit and got up early and nearly tore the house apart in her cleaning. "I just couldn't stand it any longer," she said. In the session following, the therapist accused her of giving in to her husband's demands, but she flared back, "No way! I still don't give a damn what he thinks. I cleaned it because I couldn't stand it any more." Through the paradoxical intervention she had been stimulated to redefine the situation and remove that issue from the power struggle with her husband.

There are, of course, other forms of paradoxical intervention. One is sometimes called positive attribution. In this approach the therapist relabels all of the symptoms as positive moves, altruistically motivated. For example, a husband's infidelity may be called a desperate last ditch to get his wife to pay attention to their problems. A wife's psychosomatic illness may be reinterpreted as a sacrifice of Abrahamic proportions to try to keep her family together.

We remember a couple in which the wife was having an open affair with a coworker (which she defended on the grounds of having extracted an "open marriage" contract from her husband). He spent his time in sessions being reasonable and forgiving, the long-suffering, patient spouse who loved only her and would hold on despite the pain. Finally, in one session he began for the first time to talk about his own passive-aggressive contribution to the problems they had. Immediately and without apparent provocation she launched a virulent attack on him. The therapist responded with a paradoxical response, "Why do you feel it necessary to protect him?" Both were so shocked at that comment that they couldn't think of anything to say. Finally he said, "Boy, it didn't feel like being protected to me." She said, "Are you using a paradox on us?" (she was a therapist herself and knew about these things). But the upshot was that we ended up discussing a second-level, meta rule that they had, which said that she was the strong one and had to take all of the responsibility for their problems because if his weaknesses were exposed he couldn't handle it. So she dominated every question session with unreasonable arguments in order to take the therapeutic fire.

An effective paradox must be based on an underlying truth. In the case of prescribing the symptoms, the foundational verity is that the symptom is under the control of the client. In the case of positive attribution there must be, in fact, an underlying element of nobility in the motivation of the offending partner. The result of paradoxical positive attribution is often that the couple report feeling that no one else has ever understood them so well. That is, no one else has perceived and acknowledged the altruistic component in the motivation behind the hurtful behavior.

In earlier chapters we have made reference to still another paradoxical maneuver, therapeutic sadness. This is the technique of responding to the client's stubborn refusal to respond to therapy by taking full responsibility for the failure and acknowledging that the problem has simply proved too tough for you. The sadness is all the greater because the couple clearly are good people who have a lot invested in their marriage and deserve to be happier than they have been. They came to the therapist for help and instead, after all of this work, walk away worse off than before. At least when they came they had hope; now even that has been bankrupt. The therapist reconfirms that he wants to help, has done all he could think of to help, but all to no avail. He doesn't blame them for feeling angry and disappointed (etc., etc.). Like all paradoxical intervention, this one has an element of truth in it and, speaking for ourselves, we find this a strategy of last resort because it is easy to get caught up in one's own therapeutic strategy and become as discouraged as you claim. But in fact it often results in the couple taking charge of their therapy and giving up their resistance.

When it is effective as in the case with other paradoxes, it is important not to take credit for the breakthrough. Rather, the couple should be congratulated with a full heart for having miraculously brought a virtually mortibund marriage back to life.

Other Reframing Techniques

There are an infinite number of ways to stimulate the couple to reconceptualize their situation. Most schools of psychotherapy teach their clients a whole metaphoric system by which to interpret their experiences. Psychoanalysts initiate their patients into an extensive new vocabulary and world view. Transactional analysis restructures the world in terms of internalized Parent, Adult, and Child and identifies a large number of defensive games that people play. This school of therapists is noted for using imagery that rivals any we cited in the section on dramatic imagery. These and other systems of interpretation can be effective in the hands of clinicians trained in their use. In each case, taken individually or as a group, their utility must be measured against their ability to facilitate the couple's changing in a positive way.

Another instrumentality for reframining is humor. All therapists are not equally endowed with this perspective-enlarging skill and all clients are not equally responsive to it, but when it works it is a joy to experience. We remember a couple who had had a successful series of sessions and then six months later felt they had to come back because they had lost all the ground they had formerly gained. Toward the end of the session the wife remarked with a great sigh of discouragement, "Aren't we ever going to learn how to do this by ourselves? Are we going to be coming back every six months in to our old age?"

The therapist picked up on the image and mimicked their standard quarrel using the voices and mannerisms of a very old man and woman. They began to laugh so hard that they couldn't breath. The tension was broken, a new view of the matter was provoked. They have since reported recalling that incident whenever they get discouraged and laughing at themselves and their problem. They claim that this reframing has been of great help in getting them back on track.

Whatever the means, no experienced therapist can deny that the turning point in successful therapy is very often a change of perspective brought about by a well-chosen intervention in the cognitive realm.

RESCRIPTING

Each person comes to marriage with a detailed set of expectations about what it means to be a husband and wife. This script for marital living is acquired, for the most part, unconsciously, as we grow up. We may have strong conscious convictions on some matters, but there remains a vast, taken-for-granted reservoir of expectations that we may only become aware of through experiencing the frustrations, disappointment, and even outrage that we feel when they are not met.

No couple ever married without discovering that in certain key areas their scripts for marriage did not mesh. When couples come in for marriage therapy it is almost always true that at least part of the problem that brings them is unmatched expectations. It is equally true

that a large part of problem-solving is seeing the other person's point of view. Often, with people of goodwill who are not locked into a pervasive power struggle, the correct diagnosis of the problem leads directly to the solution. This is especially true in cases in which the issue involves a *core symbol* for one partner, but something less central for the other.

Core Symbols

Richard Stuart, one of the most creative analysts of the marital state, has coined the term "core symbol" to refer to those issues which are so central to a person's script for marriage that the validity of the marital commitment itself is challenged if the symbol is violated. What constitutes a core symbol for one may mean almost nothing to another. It is not at all uncommon for one partner to do something, which according to his own script is only a minor offense, and then be absolutely astounded at his partner's "over-reaction." In the case of one couple I knew, whenever there was a major argument the young bride would pick up her things and go to her mother's house for a couple of days to "calm down." He hated it when she did this; but she reasoned that it was good to separate until tempers had cooled and they could discuss things calmly. One night, however, as their quarrel escalated and she prepared to leave, he told her:

> "If you leave, I won't be here when you come back, I have had it with your going home to mother. If you leave this time, that's it."
> "I don't even want to talk to you when you're like this," she said. "After a couple of days' cooling off, maybe we can discuss our problems without threats."
> "Ginny, I mean it. To me it's not marriage if you can't work out your own problems without running home to

mama. Unmarried people go home. Married people
hang in there. If you go, I'll know which it is for us."
She could see that he meant it. For him, leaving violated a
core symbol of marriage. For her, it was a sensible
strategy for dealing with marital quarrels.

In another case, when the husband was really angry
with his wife, he would take off his wedding ring and
throw it on the floor before stamping out of the house. To
him that was merely an expressive and harmless way to
vent his anger. To her it was symbolically a divorce. She
had wed him by putting that ring on his finger; his taking
it off in anger represented the repudiation of those vows
[Broderick, 1979a, pp. 78-79].

In cases such as this the therapist's role may be largely to
provide a setting in which each partner is able to listen and
learn about key elements in their mate's marital script. The
young woman in the illustration had no difficulty giving up
running home to mama when she fully understood how her
husband interpreted the maneuver. Similarly, when the ring-
throwing husband grasped the significance that his
"harmless" gesture had for his wife, he had little difficulty in
giving it up.

In addition to simply helping each client acquire insight into
his or her partner's symbolic world through creative listening,
some therapists find it helpful to have couples reverse roles.
For husbands and wives who have a little dramatic flair this is
an especially effective way to help each to see the marriage
from the other perspective.

The most difficult cases are those in which the partners have
scripts that are not just subtly or surprisingly different as in
the examples above, but pervasively and jarringly different.
In order to achieve joint marital scripts in these cases it may be
necessary to combine reframing and behavioral interventions.

I remember one couple who illustrated this richly. He
was stocky, bullnecked, and muscular. He looked like a
football lineman, and in the high school where they had

met, that was just what he had been. Moreover, he spoke little. When he did say something, it was likely to be blunt and to the point. He never raised his voice or seemed to get excited even when provoked. His expression might be described as stolid.

She, by contrast, was thin, angular and voluble. She had heavily rouged high cheekbones and wore pointed glasses. Her hair was teased, her clothes were frilly and on the occasion when I first saw her she was hysterical.

Her complaint was that after eleven years of marriage the romance was "dead, *dead*, DEAD!" He never spoke words of love to her, never took her out, never brought her flowers or other tokens of romantic affection. His lovemaking, "if you could call it that," was brief and neither tender nor imaginative. He was dull, selfish, rude, and totally lacking in spirituality (a quality she felt was essential in a man). In fact, he constantly humiliated her by dozing in church despite the fact that they had a minister whose sermons, everyone agreed, could have gotten a response from a stone!

For about fifteen minutes she recited his deficiencies, but he never interrupted or changed his expression from one of resigned stoicism. When she seemed to have made her point, I turned to him and said, "Well, what's your side of it? I know there are two sides to every story." He said, "I guess I don't have to tell you, do I, Doc? She's nuttier than a fruitcake." I laughed, but he said, "No, I mean it. Her father died in a nuthouse, her mother has nervous breakdowns every summer for vacation, her brother is an alcoholic, and her sister has been married four times. It runs in the family."

C. B.: But what about her feeling that you don't love her anymore—all that long list of complaints she has?
Husband: Most of them are lies.
Wife: What do you mean they're lies? When is the last time you told me you loved me?
Husband: I'll bet I tell you I love you twenty times a week.

Wife: Oh, yes. When I ask you, plead with you, "Please let me know if there is one spark of love left between us," you say, "Of course I love you; would I stay with you if I didn't love you?" But when did you ever tell me you loved me if I didn't ask you first?

Husband: There isn't time in between.

Wife: And I suppose it's a lie that you never take me out.

Husband (very quietly): I have never refused to take you out—ever. No matter how tired I am from working ten or twelve hours in the shop, I have never refused to take you out.

Wife (to counselor): Oh, yes. If I threaten to commit hari-kari, if I tell him that if I have to stay imprisoned within those dingy walls one more hour I'll go absolutely crazy, then he'll condescend to take me out. (To him) But when did you ever in our whole married life ask me to go out with you? (Bursting into tears) His idea of a big evening is to fall asleep in front of the television set. He never reads, he never listens to good music, he even hates musical comedy, and he's a damn lousy lover.

C. B. (to husband): Is that true?

Husband: She don't enjoy it anyway, so I get in and get out. Look, the fact is she's a mighty lucky woman, she don't appreciate it. I bring home every cent I make at the shop. We have a nice house with good furniture. Not many women married to a workingman have as nice a place. I don't drink up what I make like her brother, or chase women like her dad did all his life . . . , like half the men in this town do. I love my family. I'd do anything for them. I even go to her damned church with her . . . (*Wife*: Did you hear that? That's what he thinks of the Lord's Church?) . . . on the only day I have to sleep in. She likes flowery words like her minister's good at, but words are cheap! Any damn gigolo can say pretty words. I show her with actions, with everything I do, but she don't appreciate any of it.

It is clear from the dialogue that this couple have scripts for marriage that include almost no common elements. She had a long list of things that a loving husband does, and hers didn't do any of them. He had a list of what a loving husband does, and he did all of them. According to her script, she was trapped in a loveless union. According to his script, she was one of the few women in their community who had a truly devoted husband.

Once the problem was diagnosed as a case of mismatched scripts (rather than stupidity, neurosis, or selfishness), it became possible to work toward a resolution. In this particular case, I explained that the trouble was that she didn't count any of the things on his list—almost as though it were a foreign currency she wouldn't accept in her store. But in addition, he wouldn't acknowledge any of the things on her list as being legitimate tokens of love either. We began, then, by negotiating a new joint script which included items from both lists. She agreed to acknowlege the importance to her of some of the contributions he made to the relationship, and he agreed to choose from her long list some thing to do for her or with her. This was tricky, because she was quite ready to discredit any gesture on his part by saying, "You aren't doing it because you love me; you're doing it because the doctor made you." We managed to get around that by giving him quite a long list and insisting that he choose from it only things he really wanted to do, provided he found at least three per week. Both accepted this, and after only one week she came back with tears in her eyes and said, "I can't believe it. I think he really has loved me all this time" [Broderick, 1979a, pp. 80-83].

This was not the end of this couple's problems, but it surely provided a good basis for further work.

Sexual Rescripting

The concept of mismatched scripts is particularly useful in helping couples deal with sexual problems. As in other areas of life, each comes to the relationship with a lot of images and expectations about how sex ought to be and, as in other areas of life, the scripts are rarely shared, in part because they may not be very clearly spelled out in the individual's own mind.

This point was illustrated by the couple who came to me because their otherwise good marriage was marred by a sexual problem. Intercourse was painful to her; she found herself avoiding it whenever possible. Her vaginal opening, in effect, slammed shut when she was approached sexually. Her gynecologist had found no physical basis for the pain and said that she was just too tense. He advised her to relax, and prescribed a salve that would numb the vaginal orifice and so lessen the discomfort. She and her husband found this solution unsatisfactory and came to me to find out what lay at the root of the tension. When they told me their story, they also revealed that on those rare occasions when he did approach her sexually, his desire not to hurt her was so overwhelming that he often lost his erection before he could even attempt intercourse. Each felt like a failure and both felt trapped in a vicious circle which threatened to sour their relationship.

In the course of working on the problem, I had them write out their sexual scripts. It was not easy, however, for her to accept the assignment. She had been reared in a way that left her with little internal permission to speak or even to think about her sexual feelings clearly. After about twenty minutes of my most professional persuation, she finally came up with the following script:

> The greatest sexual experience I could imagine would begin with an elegant meal. I can imagine candlelight shining on the crystal. A single rose is in a vase on the table. Violins are playing in the background. Afterward we walk hand in hand in the moonlight and eventually climb marble stairs to an exquisite Louis XIV bedroom with a canopied bed. There we would undress each other, make love, and have simultaneous orgasms.

By contrast, her husband needed little urging to commit his fantasy to paper. With evident relish, he filled page after page. His script involved being awakened from a deep and innocent sleep by a naked, sex-starved female who stimulated every part of his body with every part of her body in every imaginable way (and in some ways I, at least, had never imagined). Sensation built on sensation until at last she brought both of them to a mind-boggling, earth-shaking, life-threatening mutual climax.

He was obviously pleased with his script and wondered out loud if it might have commercial possibilities. Her reaction to this story, however, was explosive. Ignoring the agreement to accept each other's scripts without offense and to discuss differences with good will, she lit into him. Didn't he realize that that woman had to do every bit of the work—that he hadn't as much as lifted a finger from beginning to end? Did he think that ideal lovemaking was just lying there on his back and letting her do it all? As far as she was concerned, he must be the "laziest, most self-centered male from the creation forward!"

This attack did not seem to ruffle him at all. He just grinned and admitted that she might be right—in fact, that all of his sexual fantasies had that same quality. For example, he might have imagined himself strolling along the street on some innocuous errand and then being ambushed by a group of teenaged nymphomaniacs, who dragged him into an alley, stripped him naked, and gang-raped him. In all of these fantasies, he played the role of the innocent bystander caught up in a whirlwind of female passion. He never felt any responsibility for what happened.

Since his further fantasies seemed to upset her even more, I intervened and asked him what he thought of her story. The question sobered him. "Do I have to tell the truth?" he asked. I nodded. "Well, frankly," he said, "after a four-hour buildup of wine and roses and violins and moonlight... who could follow an act like that? Not me! I mean, when the great moment arrives and the trumpet sounds and the spotlight goes on, I can't imagine anything I could do that wouldn't be an anticlimax."

As they each contemplated the messages of the two scripts, it became clear that at least part of their sexual problem was the result of mismatched expectations. In his script, the female did all the work and he took no responsibility or risk at all. In her script, the atmosphere did all the work and neither of them took any responsibility or risk. No wonder their sexual encounters were rare and unsatisfactory. They needed to negotiate a new joint script that involved more atmosphere for her and more risk-taking and initiative for both of them [Broderick, 1979a, pp. 140-143].

Perhaps one further illustration may serve to underscore the potential utility of script analysis in working with couples' sexual problems.

Although they were happily married and both achieved regular orgasm, she hated sex. Was it because he was an inconsiderate lover? Not at all. He was, they both agreed, one of the most considerate lovers of all time. Was it something in her background, perhaps, that had defined sex as dirty or unwholesome? No, a careful interview revealed a very positive history of healthy sexual and social development. Every avenue of inquiry ended in a blind alley. It was difficult to discover any reason at all why this couple should not be as happy in bed as out . . . until they wrote out their sexual scripts. Hers was flowing, uninhibited, and rhapsodic. His was so careful, tentative, and oversolicitous that it became apparent immediately where the problem lay. Even in his fantasy he was checking out every step with her to see if she liked it, if it felt good, if she was getting aroused. After hearing his script, she said "You know, I'd trade in a whole bucket of 'nice' for a thimble of 'go.' " For her, his overly careful approach was frustrating and irritating. But how could she complain since all he was doing was trying to please her? [Broderick, 1979b, pp. 269].

The simple awareness of his wife's perspective was all it took to motivate this husband to change his sexual approach.

ALL THE THINGS THAT CAN GO WRONG

Therapists can become dogmatic about their reinterpretations of their client's behavior. When this happens the important goals of therapy sometimes end up taking a back seat to the power struggle between client and therapist over whose view of the matter is to prevail. This is most likely to occur when the clinician is too closely wed to some particular system of therapy and has become rigid in his or her interpretation of life. But in any given case it may merely be that the symbolic world of the therapist is not much like the symbolic world of his client. Images that seem vivid and compelling to him or her may seem contrived and lacking in credibility to them. The best corrective we are aware of is letting the couple provide their own imagery. If no meeting of the minds is possible, it may be necessary to refer the couple to someone who shares their background.

Beyond this, a particular imagery, while sufficiently vivid, may offend the sensibilities of one or both clients in the same way a misaimed paradox may fall flat or have a negative effect. Although we usually have very good results with humor, more than once the witty comment that was intended to enlarge everyone's perspective instead laid an egg. On at least one occasion a client remarked, "You seem to be having a hell of a good time with our pain." When this sort of thing happens there is nothing to do but apologize and take a fresh start on a different note.

In attempting to help couples achieve joint scripts one always runs the risk that once they see clearly just how differently they view the world they will become discouraged and disillusioned rather than motivated to change. We have learned never to underestimate the capacity of a couple to rise above this initial response. Just recently a couple came in with a husband who had one of those super-charged brilliant minds that grasps everything in a second and suffers fools poorly. She, by contrast, seemed to be of only slightly above-average intelligence and, moreover, seemed almost entirely lacking in the intellectual playfulness which was his meat and drink. As the issue became painfully clear during the early sessions, he finally announced he simply couldn't live thus mismated, that he craved and required someone to interact with him on his own level. In effect he withdrew from the marriage then and there. To the therapist's surprise they kept their regular appointment the following week. Faced with the demise of her marriage, she had (miraculously, it seemed to us and to her husband) risen to dazzling heights of insight, flexible thinking, and creativity during the week. In effect, she came out of intellectual retirement. What had appeared to be relative dullness was really fatigue and stubborn resistance to playing his game.

Based on this and other similar experiences, we have developed a healthy respect for the ability of couples to confront even discouraging realities constructively. What defeats them is the mystification that fogs the relationship before the disparate scripts are spelled out.

In summary, redefining the spousal relationship is a part of virtually all marital therapy and whether it occurs as a by-product of an intervention in a behavioral or affective realm or as the result of a well calculated cognitive intervention, it is a crucial element in the achievement of therapeutic goals.

8

Changing Feelings

Feelings may change as the result of changes in behavior and perceptions. But they may also be addressed directly and transformations of behavior patterns and of world views may flow from transformations in the affective domain. Affective issues are usually introduced into triangular therapy through one or more of the following client complaints:

"I don't know how I feel."
"I don't know how my partner feels."
"I don't like how I feel."
"I don't like how my partner feels."

The first two of these call for the discovery, expression, communication, and acceptance of feelings. The second two call for efforts to replace entrenched negative feelings with more positive ones.

THE DISCOVERY, EXPRESSION, COMMUNICATION, AND ACCEPTANCE OF FEELINGS

One of Freud's most important contributions was the observation that people are often not in touch with their own feelings, particularly if their feelings are at odds with what they have been taught is right and proper. In order to avoid having to deal with these forbidden emotions, people develop all sorts of defenses, such as denying that they exist, projecting them onto others, rationalizing (that is finding more acceptable motives to explain one's actions), or somaticizing (transforming emotional tensions and pains into physical tensions and pains).

Over the years an enormous variety of techniques have been developed by various schools of therapy for helping individuals get in touch with their feelings. They range from dream analysis to psychodrama to body massage, to primal screams to hypnotism, to hitting each other with lightweight padded bats (batakas). It would not be possible to do justice to them all nor would it serve the purposes of this book. Rather, we would like to consider two or three approaches that seem to us foundational, that is, that we believe every triangular therapist ought to know how to use. Beyond these fundamentals, there is a veritable wonderland of techniques to suit every taste for those wishing to enrich their therapeutic repertoire.

Most of the techniques for getting at feelings were developed for use in individual or group sessions, but they may readily be adapted to triangular therapy provided that the laws of symmetry are not overlooked.

Reflection

Carl Rogers has done more than any other therapist to perfect the technique of uncovering feelings through the gentle confrontation of *reflection* (Rogers, 1951). It is based on the premise that we express our feelings in almost every thing we do, but often do not acknowledge or pay attention to them.

Through the technique of reflection, the sensitive therapist abstracts or distills from every cue available to him or her (that is, not only from the content of what the client says, but from the context, the facial expressions, the body posture, the tone of voice, the pace and emphasis of expression, and so forth) the feelings that appear to lie behind it. This potentially threatening confrontation is made benign by using the vocabulary of the client in framing the reflection and by phrasing it as a question rather than as an intepretation.

This technique has several benefits. First, by focusing the client's attentions on what he or she is feeling at this very moment, the therapy is automatically placed in a working mode. The agenda is here, the agenda is now. Second, holding the mirror up to him or her may be all the client needs to acknowledge feelings that are operating but not always perceived or owned. Third, if the reflection is off target in some way, the client has the opportunity to elaborate or qualify or redefine the feeling, often in the process achieving a clarity in his or her own mind, which was never previously achieved.

Beyond this, the spouse, in following this exchange, may learn much of importance about things that their partner has failed to communicate until then. And finally, the couple may learn from watching the therapist operate in this mode how to deal with each other when discussing emotional issues.

We have observed that it is easy for new clinicians to learn the external form of the Rogerian reflection, "Let me see if I understand how you feel. . . ." It is a great deal more difficult to read the flow of emotions in an ongoing session and abstract the essential, significant, underlying feelings from the multitude of things that are going on. This is difficult to convey in print since all of the subtle cues that give color to a statement are lost. Nevertheless, perhaps it would be useful to illustrate with an example the difference between a pro forma reflection and a more sensitive, effective reading and mirroring of the underlying affective issues.

> *Wife* (in a complaining tone): Then in 1978 we moved *again* to this little apartment in Nashville. I had a 3-month old baby, I didn't know a soul, and he was gone all the time.

Before proceeding the reader may wish to formulate a reflection. We have evaluated several possibilities from less to more effective.

Less Effective

I see, so in 1978 you moved to a small apartment in Nashville where you really didn't see much of your husband. Is this right?

This reflection focuses on the *events* rather than on the feelings. A series of such reflections in a row is liable to make the client feel that the therapist is hard of hearing or stupid.

A Little Better

You sound as though you were very lonely in Nashville.

This reflection does focus on a feeling (which is good), but it is a feeling that is, by now, several years in the past. If by chance, she feels equally lonely now, the therapist might get a strong response, but if it is an old issue, little real therapeutic work is accomplished by this reflection.

Still Better

It sounds as though you still have some strong feelings about this experience.

This response addresses the current feelings of the client and brings the therapy back into the here and now (which is the only place that real work can be accomplished). In our opinion, however, the experienced therapist is likely to go even a step further in picking up on the feeling included in this statement.

Most Effective

You seem to feel hurt and resentful that your husband has never been sensitive to your needs and is always wrapped up in his own affairs and leaving you to fend for yourself. Is that right?

This reflection attempts to interpret not only what is currently felt about the historic incident, but what the telling of the incident was supposed to document about the current relationship. It focuses the couple's attention on a crucial here and now issue that needs work.

It was Rogers' belief that once a set of feelings was fully experienced and owned, the biggest part of the therapist's job was done. The individual could take it from there and deal with the issue according to his or her own lights. To an extent, the same seems to be true in relationships. Once feelings are clearly communicated and understood, couples may find the rest of their task relatively straightforward and within their power to achieve with little help from the therapist.

As we indicated when discussing communication training in the chapter on behavioral change, some clinicians specialize in training couples in the art of Rogerian reflection with each other.

READING BODY LANGUAGE AND
THE MEANING OF SPATIAL POSITIONING

One special case of reflecting involves a particular focus on the language of postures and positions. When a couple comes into the office, they reveal a great deal about their feelings toward each other and also towards themselves in the way they seat themselves. It is often profitable to mirror the message of their postures and positioning to them for the same reasons that it is valuable to reflect verbal messages. A few examples may make the point more clearly.

(1) *Therapist*: I can't help noticing that you have chosen to sit as far apart as possible and have piled your coats on the cushion between you like a barrier. You (to the husband) have your whole body turned away from her and you (to the wife) seem to be all scrunched down behind that big purse of yours as though you were hiding from him. Are you really that dangerous to each other?

or

(2) *Therapist*: I notice that as we talk about this, you have your arms wrapped around yourself almost in an embrace.
Wife: It's just cold.
Therapist (nodding understandingly): I wonder if you may feel cold in two ways. This room is cold and he leaves you out in the cold so that if you want any comforting you have to hug yourself.

or

(3) *Therapist*: This seems to be a hard thing for you to listen to. As she was telling us about it your foot started tapping and you started squirming in your chair. It must take courage to stay here when you feel that uncomfortable.

or

(4) *Therapist*: I can't help noticing that you don't feel comfortable looking at me when we talk. You look at the floor, out the window, anywhere but at me. It makes me feel like a very dangerous person. Do you feel that if you looked at me I could hurt you?
Husband: I'm afraid if I looked you could see right through me.

Therapist: And what would I see if I looked right
through you? What is so terrible in there that I
shouldn't see it?
Husband: All my weaknesses.
Therapist: Ah, you are afraid that if I really got to know
you I wouldn't like you. Is that it?

It can be seen that this type of response is really just an
extension of the type of reflection demonstrated in the previous
section. It helps the couple to clarify and confront their feelings
at the moment and also trains them to be more sensitive to the
messages they send with posture and position.

In passing we might draw attention to the fact that the third
member of the therapeutic triangle, the therapist, also
communicates in this mode, whether conciously or unconsciously. Therapists, too, can gain a heightened awareness of
the messages sent by their own bodies. We have learned to pay
attention not only to externally evident cues that might be
picked up by an observer, but to those internal cues
(headaches, stiff neck, upset stomach) that may reveal to us our
own hidden feelings in a particular situation.

Perhaps no group has been more creative in devising
techniques for putting people in touch with their feelings than
the Gestaltists. (For examples of this approach see Fagan &
Shepherd, 1970, or Bockus, 1980.) Among the techniques they
have developed are *exaggeration* and *repetition*, which are
similar in form and purpose to the paradoxical techniques of
prescribing the symptom. For example, in the first case cited
in the previous section, if the therapist were a Gestaltist he or
she might very well have moved from reflection to the
assignment of an exaggeration exercise. The husband might
have been asked to turn his back fully toward his wife or to
move to a chair at the furthest extreme of the room, and she
might have been asked to hide altogether under her coat or
behind a chair. In the second case, the therapist might have
asked the woman to hug herself more tenderly and lovingly

and to say words of comfort to herself that she would like to hear from her husband.

Repitition might be used when the client expresses a feeling in a kind of a throw-away line that might otherwise almost pass unnoticed. The therapist will have him or her repeat it out loud several times, perhaps with increasing intensity. The ideal of both exaggeration and repetition is to get the feeling clearly into the awareness of both parties and to establish the experience of control over its expression.

Another whole set of awareness exercises utilizes *fantasy* in various ways. Some ask the couple to imagine themselves in various situations that are calculated to magnify important feelings much as exaggeration exercises do. There is no limit to the variety of ways that this idea can be (and has been) utilized by creative therapists.

One widely used Gestalt technique is the internal dialogue. Gestaltists believe that much human unhappiness is due to our tendency to disown parts of ourselves. As a corrective, they may set up a dialogue between the alienated parts. For example, in the case of the man who wouldn't look up at the therapist, the gestaltist might set a dialogue going between the supercritical internal judge who viewed everything he did with disapproval, and the frightened, defenseless self who was trying to hide. In the case of the woman who hugged herself, the therapist might have her comforting arms hold a conversation with her cold, lonely body.

When using this technique therapists typically have the client move back and forth between two chairs as he or she moves back and forth between the two roles. A frequently used variation of this technique might be utilized to help a person deal with grief. A distraught young woman who had suffered a miscarriage after trying to get pregnant for many months might be asked to dialogue with her lost fetus, working out her feelings of hurt and loss. Similarly, absent parents who have been unfair or rejecting or "crazy-making" can be put in the empty chair and brought into dialogue.

Some clients resist this type of exercise, but where it is accepted it can be a uniquely effective technique for uncovering and resolving internal conflicts and ambivalences.

Whenever awareness exercises are used in a triangular setting it is important not to focus so fully on one partner's feelings that the other is excluded. One approach is to assign the spectator to take notes and report his or her feelings and perspective at the end of the exercise. From the viewpoint of couple therapy this may prove to be the most important part of the session.

Satir's Maxim

People may be afraid to discover and confront their own feelings for many reasons. One of the most common fears is that once a feeling has been acknowledged, it will be acted upon. Thus, in order to control their behavior, people avoid looking at their feelings. Virginia Satir, one of the most influencial of the early family therapists, enunciated a principle that, if accepted by a client, is extremely helpful in liberating him or her from this fear. We might call it Satir's maxim (1972, ch. 7). It is, "People can experience feelings without choosing to act on them." That is, a person can get in touch with murderous urges and choose not to hurt anyone; he or she can experience strong feelings of love and sexual attraction toward another person without becoming emotionally or sexually involved with them; one can experience fear of a situation without running from it. Once the client feels secure in the knowledge that to feel and to act are separate, they gain the freedom both to acknowledge their feelings and to be in control of the active expression of them.

ALL THE THINGS THAT CAN GO WRONG

It is undeniable that a person takes a greater risk in revealing his or her feelings in a triangular situation than when alone with a therapist. The professional, after all, is not personally involved in the relationship and can afford a detached, nonjudgmental, accepting posture no matter how negative the feelings expressed might be. It is not so with the spouse. An important part of one's life is tied up in one's marriage and it is inevitable that some kinds of messages from one's mate can be devastating. It is hard to imagine a husband or wife who would be unmoved in hearing their mate say, "I never really loved you—even at first," or, "Frankly, and I'm sorry if this hurts you, but you're just not very bright," or "You have become a tub of lard; your body disgusts me," or even, "I have come to hate you and everything about you." Even couples who indulge in this kind of exchange on a regular basis are wounded in the process.

When these kinds of statements come out in a session there are basically two strategies for dealing with them, depending on the therapist's reading of the overall context. He or she can attempt to soften the impact of it in one of several ways or, if the situation calls for it, he or she may choose to help the couple deal with this bold emotional fact and its implications without any cushioning at all.

Softening the Blow

First, it should be emphasized that the therapist should only attempt to cushion the impact of a negative statement if in so doing he or she feels that the hurtful expression in fact misrepresents the real nature of the bonding felt by the other person. Often people make statements in the heat of the moment that are purposefully phrased to be hurtful (rather than accurate) or which are poorly phrased so that they communicate a different message (or a different degree of feeling) than was intended, or which express only one part of an ambivalent or complex feeling, leaving the other more reassuring part unexpressed.

Where the statement seems to be designed to be hurtful, the therapist might ask, "Do you really mean that?" thus eliciting the explanation. Better still, he or she might reflect the metamessage, "You have hurt me and I want to hurt you," or "You pay no attention to my feelings at all unless I get desperate and even brutal." This refocuses the couple's attention on the process of their interaction rather than on the unpalatable content of the message. By putting it in perspective its destructive consequences are reduced by some degree.

In the case where the therapist senses that the individual has inadvertently expressed his or her feelings in a manner that is more absolute or cruel or destructive than was intended, it is often possible to restate the meaning in a less threatening and more accurate form. For example, when the husband told his wife he had never really loved her, a sensitive therapist might rephrase the statement, "Everything has been so terrible between you in recent months that it is hard to remember or believe there was ever any positive feeling there," or, "I feel so bruised I cannot bring myself to admit to any positive feelings that might open me up to further hurt."

The third case, in which the attacking statement reflects only the negative part of an ambivalent feeling, can be handled by giving voice to the more complex emotional reality. "You say you hate him and everything about him, yet here you are trying to work out your problems. It sound to me like you wouldn't feel so hurt and angry if underneath you didn't care."

It is also useful to comment upon the style of communication that leads to what we have sometimes called "killer" statements and to suggest that there are more effective ways to share feelings with a partner. Reframing and also behavior modification techniques described in earlier chapters may appropriately be brought into play at this point.

Confronting the Blow Head On

Sometimes it does not seem appropriate to try to soften the impact of an emotional zinger. Rather, the therapist helps the couple to confront the reality of the negative feelings expressed. "She says she doesn't love you, Bill, where do you go from there?" or "Boy, that statement would take all of the wind out of my sails. I don't think I would know what to do next. How *are* you dealing with this, Bill?" However grim the scene that follows, it is better played out in the presence of a mediator than in another setting.

Catharsis Versus Restraint

There are certain schools of therapy that see great virtue in stimulating couples to express all of their hostile and hurtful feelings forthrightly and without worrying too much about hurting the other person. The rationale is twofold. First, it is held that the person expressing the feeling is relieved to be able to express it and that once expressed, the feeling itself is diminished in intensity. This is contrasted to the effects of bottling up feelings that, left without a means of expression, grow in destructive potential until they manifest themselves in physical symptoms or explosive destructiveness. Second, it is held that relationships can only become authentic and intimate when they can accommodate that kind of cathartic expression.

It appears, however, that this philosophy is ill-founded. Empirical research (Strauss, 1974) and, increasingly, clinical opinion (Ellis, 1976; Mace 1976) support the opposite conclusion, namely, that couples fare better if they exercise restraint and employ civility in their interaction. Openly hostile attacks, far from resulting in diminished feelings of resentment, in fact breed more hostility. Anger and other negative emotions feed upon themselves when expressed, rather than draining away, as the cathartic theory holds.

As we have stated earlier, feelings need to be expressed and communicated, but in nonattacking ways. One of the most helpful of all interpersonal skills is the ability to let someone know of one's needs or hurts in such a way as to recruit a partner rather than to create an enemy.

Triadic Inhibition

An opposite problem in dealing with feeling in triangular therapy grows out of the inhibition many clients feel about

expressing negative feelings in front of their partner. They
fear, not without justification, that anything they say may be
held against them. One solution is to see the partners
separately. This permits each to vent their fears and doubts
and resentments without burdening the partner with the pain
of hearing it all. What it fails to accomplish is to teach the
couple how to deal with their important feelings in the
relationship. For this reason we prefer to work in the
triangular format. In this format it is the therapist's job to
make the setting as safe as possible. One of the chief means of
doing this is seeing to it that hurtful expressions are dealt with
in the session so that no potentially dangerous unsettled
business is left over to take home. When this is not possible,
some couples volunteer to hold off discussion of a sensitive topic
until the next session. Eventually, of course, the object is to
teach the couple how to deal with any issue that might come up
without third-party intervention.

HELPING COUPLES LET GO OF
ENTRENCHED NEGATIVE FEELINGS

In the natural order of things, relationships that have
suffered wounds through hurt, neglect, or betrayal gradually
heal without outside help. The chief ingredient of restoration is
time itself, together with whatever remnants of pair
commitment and mutual goodwill survived the trauma. When
couples seek professional help, it is generally because this
natural process has been blocked. The therapist's part is to
help them find a way to let go of entrenched negative feelings
toward each other and get a positive emotional economy
flowing again.

In earlier chapters we have considered some of the most
effective means of achieving this shift. Behavioral interventions, which help the couple to flood the relationship with
positive experiences, are particularly potent. Cognitive
interventions too may play a crucial role. Changing the way a
couple perceives each other is often a prerequisite to changing

the ways they feel toward each other. Also, as we have seen in the previous section of the present chapter, simply clarifying, owning, and communicating unwelcome feelings may diminish their potency and lead to their replacement with more positive emotions.

There are times, however, when none of these approaches seems to be enough. One or both clients seems locked into an almost compulsive fear or anger or mistrust that resists all attempts at ameliorization. Love, trust, and forgiveness seems to be beyond their capacity to achieve. In such cases we have experienced some success through the use of one or both of the following strategies. One is *partitioning the pain*, the other, *charasmatic restructuring*.

Partitioning the Pain

When feelings are particularly resistant to change it is often because they are deeply rooted in the person's life history. Commonly, the unhappy events that have triggered the current difficulty are painfully reminiscent of traumatic events in the person's early family life and also of wounds suffered earlier in the present relationship (or even in an earlier marriage). It is as though all of the significant relationships in one's life have, one after another, confirmed and reinforced the lesson of the previous hurt.

Let us consider briefly the cases of the following three "stuck" clients.

> Robert, I have forgiven you for the infidelity; I have forgiven you for making love to my best friend while I was suffering in the hospital. As hard as it has been, God knows that I have forgiven you. But don't expect me to forget it. I wish I could, but I don't think those images will ever leave me. And I don't see how you can expect me ever to feel the same toward you as I used to before that happened.

> I'm sorry Marilyn. I don't hate you and I don't love you. I just don't feel anything at all for you. Nothing. I am

numb. I wish it wasn't that way but it is and you just can't squeeze something out of nothing.

I know it hurts you to have me say this, but so help me, I can't help it. Michael, I am terrified of you. I know it is not your fault. You never hit me or anything, but I start getting nervous every day when it starts to get time for you to come home and by the time I hear your car in the driveway, I am so tense that it's all I can do to keep from running out the back door. I really can't explain it. There's no real reason but I'm just terrified of you.

In the first of these cases it is not at all surprising that this woman would have great difficulty in dealing with the double betrayal of her husband and her best friend. Even a couple with everything going for them might reasonably be expected to take a long time to work through all of the feelings of mistrust and hurt and anger on one side and the guilt and shame and resentment on the other. But if one discovers that this woman grew up with a father who repeatedly cheated on her mother and that her own first marriage ended by her husband's leaving her for another woman . . . it is easy to imagine how profound her mistrust of men must have become. If she is to have any chance at all of dealing constructively with the situation in her current marriage, she needs first to find a way to differentiate it from her earlier experiences. She must be helped (probably in private sessions) to deal with the pain she experienced as a child and then with the trauma of her first husband's infidelity and abandonment. Only when these have been separated out can she profitably attempt to renegotiate the marital bond with her husband. Incidently, if her therapist should happen to be a male it would be prudent to consider with her whether her present mistrust of men is so great that it would make sense to have her work with a woman therapist.

In the case of the husband who has come to feel nothing at all, neither love nor anger, toward his wife, it might be appropriate to ask how he learned to deal with pain in that way. The probability is that either his mother or father (or both) modeled this approach, forbidding themselves (and their children) any direct expression of negative feelings, and reverted instead to passive strategies such as withholding or withdrawal. Or, it is possible that he came from a highly conflicted home and learned to survive by beoming numb to the pain he experiences there. Whatever the case, it is of value to examine the origins and utilities of such a strategy. In doing so, it is redefined. Instead of accepting it as an indication of truly feeling nothing, the numbness is identified as an indication of feeling too much.

It would also not be surprising to discover that this husband has felt that his needs and feelings have never been listened to or responded to in the marriage. Even though he may be partly responsible for this, since he is not overly articulate in expressing his needs, he still may feel that it has not paid to be open or vulnerable. This old business may need to be dealt with before the current new business can be successfully addressed.

Finally, in the case of the woman who is frightened of her husband, apparently without cause, it is equally clear that the roots of the fear need to be partitioned between her growing-up experiences (which are almost certain to have been horrendous), her earlier hurts in the relationship with her husband, and those things he does currently that threaten her. As in the other cases, each component may well call for a different type of intervention.

Charismatic Restructuring

There is another type of intervention that we have observed to be effective in inducing a shift from destructive to constructive feelings in a relationship. We have called it *charismatic restructuring*. It consists of the therapist virtually infecting the client couple with his or her own confidence, energy, and optimism. Some therapists come by this quality naturally; other have to work at it (and for some, it may be counter to their personal style). In effect the therapist sweeps the couple past their stuck spot by virtue of his or her own enthusiasm and persuasiveness. Of course, enthusiasm itself is not a substitute for diagnostic skill nor for clinical sophistication, but it is effective in helping some couples turn the corner.

ALL THE THINGS THAT CAN GO WRONG

Despite all of the many resources that therapists have for helping couples to change their feelings, some clients will not choose to do so. Out of fear or stubbornness or, perhaps in some cases, out of shrewd insight into their mate's character and trustworthiness, they refuse to give up their negativism. This is their right. Whatever the therapist's personal view of the potential of the relationships, only the people in the marriage can judge whether it is worth it to open up the flow of positive exchange again or not. With intimacy comes risk. The risk is real and it is not for outsiders to make the decision as to whether the probability of benefits offsets the possibility of further destructive hurt.

Our job ends with making the choice real.

9

Dissolving the
Therapeutic Triangle

The object of triangular therapy, of course, is not to have the therapist become a permanent feature of the client's marriage. Rather, it is to join with the pair in working toward some jointly agreed-upon goals and then, the task accomplished, to withdraw. We have spent several chapters observing how one effectively may join a couple, and several additional chapters on how one effectively may help a couple select and achieve therapeutic goals. In this chapter we wish to consider how one may effectively disengage when the work is done.

In one sense, termination may be viewed as the final step in the sequence of therapeutic processes. In another sense the process of termination may be seen as beginning in the first minute of the first session. When a triangular relationship aborts prematurely after only one or two meetings or dribbles to a slow extinction through a series of missed appointments, one may be certain that the roots of the problem lie in the failure to accomplish the initial tasks of therapy.

It is equally true, though perhaps less obvious, that when a triangle gets stuck and the sessions drag on for months without real progress taking place, this too is likely to be the result of ineffective rapport, diagnosis, and goal selection.

Still, there are certain issues particular to the final stages of therapy. In Parson's paradigm of the therapeutic process, the task of the final stage is to reinforce the changes achieved in earlier stages, to establish the new perspectives and patterns of interaction as permanent features of the couple's life together.

The first task of this chapter, then, is to review the process of successful termination. The second will be to look at all the things that can go wrong and how one might respond in each case.

THE DECISION TO TERMINATE

When the course of therapy runs smoothly, termination seems to occur as a natural culmination of all that has come before. The very process of clarifying goals in the early sessions makes it easy to tell that they have been substantially achieved later on. In the simplest case what usually happens is something like this: After a series of good weeks (that is, weeks in which they have experienced progress toward their goals) the couple finds they don't have much to discuss in the session. This is not a certain sign in itself, since it is possible that they are simply working through a plateau period, digesting what they have accomplished already before tackling the next therapeutic task. But if it appears that they have achieved most of the goals they have set for themselves and have demonstrated to each other and to the therapist that they can operate as a competent problem-solving unit, it is likely that a slow or merely sociable session should be read as a sign of approaching termination.

Typically the couple will bring up the issue of dissolving the therapeutic relationship themselves. People do this in a variety of ways. Some, after a protracted pause, will report that in the car on the way to the appointment they were discussing whether they weren't about ready to finish up. Some spend part of the session reviewing their progress and expressing their appreciation for all the therapist has done to help them. Some say abruptly at the end of the session that they don't feel they need to come back next week.

If the signs are all present, but the couple seem reluctant to bring the subject up the therapist will usually comment on how much they have achieved and ask how they would be able to tell if they were finished. This gives them permission to suggest termination without fear of offending the therapist. It also gives them an opportunity to review their goals to see if there are any additional issues they wish to deal with before terminating.

As a matter of policy we always explicitly make every termination an open one. That is, the couple is told that they are able to come back next week or the next year if additional issues come up. Some do just that. In our view one of the marks of a successful termination is that the client can come back for a retread without apology or any sense of failure.

Frequently, although the couple recognize that the time has come for them to try it alone, they feel some anxiety. They are mistrustful of their newly acquired skills and perspectives. Their fear is that as soon as the therapist is out of the picture they will return to their earlier unhappy ways.

The simplest response to this is to schedule one or more follow-up sessions three or four weeks down the road. They know they can come in sooner if they really need to so that they need not fear being cast off cold turkey. Many times things will go so well that the couple will cancel the follow-up sessions with a note that reports on how well things are progressing. Others use the sessions to report on progress, work out misunderstandings, and increase their confidence that this is going to work.

In cases where the couple's anxiety about separation prevents triangular termination, we negotiate a schedule of gradual disengagement. If we have typically met with them weekly we shift to every other week, then to once a month. This program gives them the opportunity to practice their new skills on their own for increasing periods of time. Soon enough, this couple also will feel that the need for the extra support is past—at least for the time being. The knowledge that they can return when they want to makes it easier not to have to.

Where these strategies are insufficient to shake loose fearful or overdependent clients, it seems likely that the therapist has unwittingly entered into an inappropriately enmeshed relationship with the couple. In a later section of the chapter we will discuss what needs to be done in such cases.

Termination by Contract

Some clients know from the first session when their final session will be. Certain sex therapists (e.g., Masters and Johnson), behaviorists (e.g., Richard Stuart), and conciliation courts (e.g., the pioneering one in Los Angeles) contract with the couple for a set number of sessions. When the series is complete, the therapy is over. Although we are more comfortable with a more flexible approach, there is much to be said for structuring the therapy in such a way that the couple expects to complete their task in a set time. The deadline itself doubtless provides an important therapeutic function. People pace themselves to the time they know they have contracted for. In some of these settings additional time can be negotiated when circumstances dictate.

Since the time of termination is not tied to an evaluation by the couple that their goals have been met, it is especially important for therapists who use this approach to build an evaluative procedure into their program. In fact, it is our opinion that setting arbitrary limits on the number of sessions can only be justified if it can be demonstrated that most couples can achieve their goals within the framework. Probably, as with other therapeutic approaches, this one selectively attracts those couples who are most likely to be responsive to its features. All of the programs listed as examples in the previous paragraph (and many other similar programs) have produced strong research evidence that they are effective for most of the couples who come to them.

ALL THE THINGS THAT CAN GO WRONG

All of the things that can go wrong in the termination phase of therapy may be grouped into three broad categories: *premature termination, bogging down,* and *avoiding the dissolution of the triangular bond.*

Premature Termination

When we speak of a termination being premature we imply two things: first, that the therapeutic relationship was dissolved before any significant goals had been met, and second, that if the therapy had continued it was reasonable to expect that progress toward the client's goals might have been made. We exclude from this category cases that are terminated by joint agreement after only one or two sessions because it becomes clear to all parties that the help needed might be best sought from some other source. The ethical obligation of the therapist is to provide an appropriate referral and a lot of support for the couples choosing to seek out a different form of help.

For the most part, when a triangular relationship aborts early it is because the therapist was not able to establish symmetrical rapport with the couple. Sometimes, when it is only one member who is left unconnected, the more easily reached partner may stay on as a single client. The therapist should be aware (and should make the clients aware) that this sort of situation is fraught with peril for the marriage, although it may be useful for the individual. What is likely to happen is that the partner in therapy will develop more and more positive self regard as a result of the growth produced and become increasingly unwilling to put up with an insensitive or abrasive or withholding spouse. Also, the courage to confront the possibility of separation may be strengthened, even though the therapist in no way pushes for this outcome.

Of course life events having nothing to do with the therapy itself may be the major factor in dropping out before work can be accomplished. Financial or health problems or other family crises may intervene and distract the couple from their own relationship and its problems. But by and large, we feel that a premature termination is symptomatic of therapist failure at the early tasks of triangular therapy. Rapport was not established, the diagnosis was not on target or was presented in a fashion that frightened or offended the couple. No common goals were able to be established or the intervention techniques were inappropriate or offensive. In effect, the clients are registering a vote of no confidence in the therapeutic process. Despite the possibility of legitimate exceptions, a therapist who loses any major fraction of his or her cases in this fashion owes it to him or herself and to the clients to seek out supervision or consultation to determine what is going awry.

Bogging Down

Opposite to premature termination is the problem of getting bogged down in interminable sessions where no discernible progress occurs over a period of weeks and even months. Probably every therapist ought to allow himself or herself a substandard session once in a while, and two in a row with the same client is not unheard of even in the best therapeutic circles, but by the time a third session comes and goes without any appreciable movement, the therapist owes it to himself or herself and to the client to evaluate the situation very carefully.

Is the therapist locked in some sort of a power struggle with the couple or one of its members? Does the diagnosis need to be reconsidered and a new therapeutic contract negotiated? Is a more assertive intervention called for to help this couple get off the mark? There are endless possibilities.

Although it is often possible to break out of these doldrums just by reviewing the case, in our experience it is much faster and surer to seek consultation with a colleague. It is often humiliating to discover how quickly an outsider can diagnose the problem in the triangle. It is all a matter of perspective. By definition, a blind spot is invisible to the person who has it.

Recently, I referred a young couple to a younger colleague after months of frustrating nonprogress. They immediately started doing better. In consultation it became clear that somehow in my work with them I had fallen into a parental role and pulled a lot of passive-aggressive resistance from this young couple, who had had years of practice in dealing with parents in that way. The younger therapist was able to escape that trap and establish a working, collegial relationship from the first session.

In another incident, an attractive woman trainee seemed to be stuck in her work with a couple. Watching video tapes of the session suggested to her supervisor that the male member of the pair was strongly attracted to her and the female member was jealous and yet felt reluctant to bring it up because the therapist hadn't done anything obvious to evoke it. The supervisor joined the session one day and helped the three of them work it through. Without some help it is difficult to see how they could have resolved the problem, since the couple was unwilling to bring the issue up and the therapist was not fully aware of what was going on due to a blind spot of her own.

Secrets

One potential cause of getting stuck is the presence of a secret that is crucial to the issues being worked on, but is not brought into the session. Sometimes it is a secret shared by the couple but not the therapist (for example, that they have a developmentally retarded child at home or that the wife is an alcoholic or that the husband had a homosexual affair early in their marriage). They may have agreed to leave this out of the sessions or it may be simply a matter of trying to put their best foot forward to the therapist. Whatever the reason, the only cure that we know of is for the therapist to sniff it out. Usually there are a number of clues over a period of time (glances at each other when certain issues come up, evasiveness in dealing with questions, lots of "I don't knows"). Beyond that there is a sense that the equation of the relationship just doesn't balance. There is more pain or resentment or discouragement or commitment than can be accounted for by the known facts. Like astronomers who may detect the presence of an undiscovered planet by its effect on the orbits of other planets, so a sensitive therapist may be able to observe that something crucial is missing from the official story.

Perhaps the most straightforward policy is the best. The couple (or individual) can be confronted with the observation that some piece seems to be missing from the puzzle and that without it, everything seems to be bogged down. For detective mystery lovers, of course, it is most satisfying to put all of the clues together and then in a dramatic moment confront them with, "Why don't you tell me about the abortion, Mrs. Dobbs?" It must be admitted that the response when one is correct is most gratifying. On the other hand, few things are more embarrassing than to build up to one of these Agatha Christie moments of truth and then turn out to be absolutely wrong.

Among the most damaging secrets are those shared between one partner and the therapist. Typical is the secret that one mate is currently (or recently) enmeshed in an affair. For one thing, becoming party to this or any other guilty secret places therapists in the role of coconspirator if they keep the confidence. Yet to breach the confidence is to alienate the guilty spouse. Different therapists deal with this in different ways. Some refuse adamantly to share any guilty secrets, threatening to tell all they know if they are ever burdened with such confidences. Others keep the confidence, but insist that the affair be broken off if the therapy is to continue (on the grounds that the couple needs to concentrate on its own relationship in order to profit from the current therapeutic work).

We are less doctrinaire, attempting to deal with each case according to its merits, but we acknowledge that it is a therapeutic problem. From our point of view, one of the best responses is to persuade the guilty party to share the secret with the spouse and work on dealing with the fallout. Judgement must be used in individual cases, however.

Therapist Burn-Out

Sometimes a therapist cannot avoid noticing that an increasing portion of his or her case load is stuck. Moreover, work is getting to be less and less rewarding and more and more taxing. It becomes increasingly difficult to concentrate on what is going on in a session. Cancellations are welcomed with a sense of relief or even celebration.

These are the symptoms of professional burn-out, a phenomenon observed in many demanding professions. Recently a number of books and articles on the burn-out phenomenon have been published. In our opinion it is a symptom of a poor emotional economy. That is, it is the result of a chronic imbalance between what one puts into one's practice and what one gets out of it. If this diagnosis is correct, then to avoid emotional bankruptcy as a therapist one must either decrease the expenditure of energy or increase the return. There are a number of things to consider in attempting to establish a sound emotional economy.

Pace

In every area of life one of the marks of a true professional is that they have mastered the art of pacing themselves so that they never run out of steam before the job at hand is done. In athletics, in business, and in life it is the overzealous beginner who is most likely to commit all of their reserves of energy early in the contest and then fade in the stretch. It is so in therapy. Inexperienced clinicians are likely to work too hard in each session and worry too much between sessions. Often we tell trainees, "Have you noticed that you are working harder than the couple in this session? Relax! The idea is to get them to work on the relationship, not for you to do it for them." We are suggesting that it is not simply a case of more experienced therapists losing their enthusiasm. The best therapy, in our opinion, is done by seasoned professionals who efficiently monitor the amount of energy they put into each hour so that they do not come up short before the day is over.

Probably a major element in burn-out is resentment about the unrelentingness of the demands of the profession. Pacing can reduce those feelings by establishing the therapist's control over his or her own working rhythm. For example, the therapist may wish to become more assertive in protecting the ten minutes between sessions, lunch and dinner hours, and at-home time from being gobbled up by client importunity. Learning to communicate expectations firmly and not being afraid to set limits and to say "no" are important skills for our clients to learn, and no less so for ourselves. It is important, not only that our lives be well paced, but that we feel ourselves in firm control of the pace.

Fueling

It is easy for therapists to fall into the same trap that their clients often do and to find that they are paying too little attention to their own emotional fueling. Undernourishment in either one's professional or one's personal life can contribute to burn out.

There are three professional resources that a therapist should jealously maintain. First, to keep from going stale it is important to read and attend workshops on various aspects of the field. Through these means fresh ideas, new perspectives, and creative techniques are constantly being fed into one's repertoire. Second, participation in professional organizations and their meetings adds the dimension of community. Third, maintaining a place in an informal network of therapists with whom you discuss difficult or interesting cases can, with the other resources, make the difference between isolation and professional stagnation on the one hand, and a satisfying, growing career experience on the other. Still another important protection against burn out is variety in one's client load. While it is worthwhile to specialize, in our opinion, each therapist owes himself or herself a balanced diet. Seeing mostly couples with overweight, depressed wives or with impotent husbands with a sex-role conflict or who are going through a divorce can be especially draining. Change of fare may be as important as pace itself. A therapist who mostly sees couples may wish to start a couple's group or bring in the children of some of his or her clients or in some other way help himself or herself out of the rut. We firmly believe that this will be doubly helpful for the clients. Not only will it regenerate energy in their therapist, but the variety may also result in an increase in energy in their relationship.

Despite the interpersonal skills that we develop as professionals, it may also happen that we fail to utilize them in behalf of important relationships in our own lives. Many of us have become so absorbed in building our careers that our personal lives have fallen into disrepair. When this occurs we find ourselves without the crucial emotional nourishment that those relationships can provide when they are functioning well. Thus another root of professional burn-out may be relational neglect in the private sector of our lives. This will be dealth with at greater length in the final chapter of this book.

Humor

Whatever the reason, when one finds oneself losing one's appetite for therapy, a helpful antidote is to introduce more humor into the therapeutic transaction. In an earlier chapter we noted that humor-rich interpretations often stimulated clients to reframe their situations in helpful ways. It may be equally effective in helping the therapists reframe their own situations. Humor, besides providing a benign metaperspective, introduces new energy and variety into the therapeutic triangle. At least one author has suggested that this is a central component in successful treatment of therapist burn-out.

Avoiding the Dissolution of the Triangular Bond

A third major problem in termination, which can be differentiated from prematurity and from getting stuck, is when the termination is actively avoided because of the interdependency that has developed between the therapist and the couple.

As with families who cannot launch their children, these enmeshed therapeutic triangles are likely to be caught in a web of strong ambivalent bonds. In some cases the negative components are most in evidence and the sessions are full of confrontation and conflict. Yet if one of the three or an outsider pushes to end the triangular relationship, the effort is quickly and effectively sabotaged.

Perhaps more frequently, the positive side of the effect is more in evidence. The clients continually express their appreciation for the therapist and for all they have accomplished, and the therapist in turn is fulsome in his or her warmth toward them. But let someone suggèst the time has come to terminate and one or another will do something outrageous that has to be dealt with in future sessions.

The dynamics of this sort of overdependency may be quite complex in specific instances. On the couple's side they may come to view the therapist as a powerful stabilizing influence on the runaway destructiveness of their relationship. Like the one-eyed man in the land of the blind the therapist may become, not king, but captive—too valuable to be allowed to escape.

Or, the therapist may fall into the role of warm, supportive parent to a couple who never had one in either of their growing-up experience. They may, understandably, be reluctant to give up such a wonderful compensatory relationship, once achieved. Or, more problematic still, they may triangulate the therapist as surrogate parent into some unresolved conflict left over from their youths. Many other possibilities also exist.

On the other side, the therapist may become seduced into this enmeshed relationship because of his own unfinished business with his own parents or siblings or children. Or possibly it is just irresistible to be this important to someone. Whatever the case, it is the therapist, as the professional in the group, who has the obligation to identify and deal with the problem when it occurs.

Obviously, the best treatment is prevention. Well-trained therapists will work hard to focus upon and sponsor the couple's relationship with each other rather than with them. They avoid interventions that have the metamessage, "I am wise and powerful . . . . you are weak and ignorant." Instead, they will continually reinforce a definition of the triangular relationship that identifies them as the temporary, dispensable, auxiliary member and the couple as the central, enduring, problem-solving core unit. When this is successfully accomplished, termination flows smoothly from therapy. When this is not achieved and the triangle becomes enmeshed, it will almost certainly take an outside consultant or supervisor to unhook the members from one another.

Theoretically, entangled therapists could diagnose their own dilemmas and effect the disengagement without outside help. In practice this is extremely difficult. Outsiders have the detached metaperspective that is required to guide the differentiation. They are in the best position to choose the strategy that will break up the over-bonded system.

SUMMARY

We have seen that most of the things that go wrong in the termination stage of therapy are really indications that things have gone wrong in the course of the therapy itself. Clinicians will find no more reliable diagnostic indicator of how effective their therapy is than how their cases terminate. Since this is so, it is every therapist's professional obligation to monitor his or her cases carefully, and to take responsibility for what he learns in the process.

If a recurrent pattern of premature termination becomes evident he or she may be certain that he or she needs to tune up skills in the area of establishing symmetrical rapport and of negotiating a mutually acceptable triangular contract. The diagnostic task is more complex if the system is getting stuck. A variety of factors might be responsible. We have suggested that he or she will do well to look at the possibility of having become locked in a power struggle with one or both of the clients. Perhaps he or she needs to reconsider the diagnosis of the couple's problem or select a more effective strategy of intervention. He or she ought also to consider the possibility that there may be a secret that prevents the couple from addressing the real issues. Beyond these specifics each therapist needs to look honestly at the issue of burn out, and if it is operative, do what can be done to revive his or her flagging investment in therapy.

Finally, we have discussed the unhappy case when the therapist finds himself or herself triangled into the couple's problems in a way that sabotages both progress and termination. In that case we have strongly recommended seeking outside consultation.

In summary, there is no clearer indicator of a therapist's professionalism and ethical commitment than how he or she handles problematic terminations.

•

10

Physician, Heal Thyself

•   •

Critics of the marital therapy profession have sometimes
asserted that "most of them can't even keep their own
marriage together, what makes them think they could help
anybody else?" I am not aware of any data comparing the
marital stability of therapists to other groups in society. It is
indisputable, however, that divorces and other unhappy
outcomes occur among us. Our professional expertise does not
seem to prevent failure in our own relationships. Indeed, it
might be argued that receiving training as a marital therapist
puts many marriages under considerable strain.

In the first section of this chapter we wish to review some
features of our profession that do in fact increase the strain in
our marriages. Next, we will look at mechanisms for
converting our training into a marital resource rather than a
handicap. Finally, we have a few observations to make on how
single, divorced, and unhappily married therapists may deal
with these issues so that they do not detract from their
professional effectiveness.

WARNING:
THE PRACTICE OF MARITAL THERAPY
MAY BE DANGEROUS TO YOUR MARITAL HEALTH

To begin with, it should be admitted that this profession attracts candidates who may already be more likely than a random sample to have marital problems. In fact, a survey of our own pool of trainees over the years reveals them to have, as a group, personality profiles that are very similar to those of our clinical clientele. Both are different from the average person on the street and from the type of client that comes in for individual counseling.

The qualities that characterize a great many marriage therapists and their clients are (1) a high level of interpersonal need or dependency (this person is sensitive to people and their approval and has a greater than average need for strokes from significant others); (2) a resentment of authority and restrictive societal rules; (3) a history of hurts received in intimate relationships starting in childhood; (4) a tendency to utilize the defense mechanism of denial, that is, putting a good face on things as a means of dealing with problems.

On the face of it, it would appear that these qualities may predispose a person to have their problems in the area of relationships rather than other major areas of their life. It may very well be that painful relational experiences heighten one's consciousness to the potential of professional solutions. Also, such experience textures a person's life. I have had the experience of trying to train individuals as therapists whose lives had been so bland as to leave them untextured. They simply could not seem to figure out what was going on in complex relationships. It has sometimes seemed that in order to be a good relationship therapist there needs to have been some time in one's life when it was a matter of survival to learn to discern what was going on in one's family—to read it right so as to respond to it right. The best therapists seem to be those who have developed this capacity, but whose personal situations has improved, so that at this point they are free to retire these antennae from personal service and place them in the service of their clients.

Another element that may account for some of the similarity between therapists and clients is that a substantial minority of therapists are recruited into the field from the pool of clients. In the course of therapy some of them develop a real knack for self-diagnosis and sensitive restructuring of relational patterns. With or without the sponsorship of their therapist one or both may go on to get clinical training. It is little wonder that at least this subset of trainees have problems similar to those of their clients.

So, the first point is that part of the strain in marital relations observed among fledgling therapists may be a matter of preselection. I am convinced, however, that the chief factor in marital strain among trainees is introduced unwittingly through the training process itself.

The Hazards of Asymmetrical Resocialization

In the course of becoming a marital therapist the candidate is not merely exposed to learning new skills and concepts, he or she is virtually resocialized. That is, we attempt to teach trainees a new world view, a new conceptual paradigm of reality with new axioms of cause and effect, a new vocabulary, a new value system, and a new style of interpersonal interaction. The therapeutic world is founded upon existential values. The ultimate good is held to be individual growth and self-actualization (not loyalty), assertiveness (not self-sacrifice), differentiation (not commitment), and openness (not privacy). These values are promoted without apology or debate. They are held to be self-evident. Yet they are not the only viable set of values. In fact, there is a substantial possibility that as the trainee gradually adopts these values he or she will come into conflict with the more traditional value premises upon which their marriage was originally based. When this occurs one's spouse and also other relatives and friends are liable to resist the new interpretations of reality and the new priorities. New converts to any faith are notorious proselytizers and while this sometimes results in a general shift in a person's network toward a more existential world view, it is at least equally common for it to result in strain and conflict. Unfortunately, most programs do not deal directly with this issue and so the trainee is not given the conceptual tools to identify and deal with the problems that may arise. Resistance among one's network is likely to be interpreted as insensitivity and stubbornness. In the case of one's spouse it is easy for this feeling to lead to the conclusion that one is mismatched in important and substantial ways.

Beyond this basic shift in general values, the trainee is systematically taught a set of new relationship scripts. A high value is placed upon communicating feelings openly and fully, processing interactions, sharing perceptions, achieving equality and mutuality, confronting problems directly, and so forth. In many cases this new script differs substantially from the more traditional script upon which the marriage was established. The partner may well resent the new demands, the unnegotiated shift in values. He or she may not wish to discuss feelings, may wish to avoid confrontations, may want to retain established patterns of interaction.

It is easy for this to develop into the classic power struggle or vicious circle. The trainee, with all the best motivations, commits himself or herself to try to reeducate their spouse; the spouse holds out for the way things used to be. Animated attempts to share all the exciting things that are going on at the training center are met with indifference and inattention; books and articles that are brought home (and underlined and left next to the toilet) remain unread; there is no enthusiasm to "just try" the new style of communication or of negotiating differences or of interpreting dreams or of making love. The trainee persists, driven by the dark fantasy that if the spouse doesn't come around the marriage will become sterile and oppressive. The spouse digs in with the conviction that if you give an inch you end up in some therapeutic land of Oz where every dream is analyzed, every sexual encounter rated, every motive challenged, and every facet of the relationship overexamined.

At the same time that this strain is being introduced into one's marital relationship, one is having a variety of intense and engaging group experiences with other trainees. These colleagues, new converts like oneself, are likely to be far better models of the new virtues than one's resistant spouse. In that setting one may share emotional heights and depths, insights, and intimacies that exceed any ever shared in the marital context. The group, with its emphasis on individual growth and experience, is not likely to be overly protective of the marital bond with the absent, nonparticipating spouse. Commonly they encourage sharing of information and feelings that, if the spouse know of them, would be seen as a betrayal of the privacy of the marriage. In many settings touching and hugging and sharing of sexual fantasies are encouraged (or even arranged). In some unhappy cases these familiarities have led to still greater intimacies outside of the group setting. It is small wonder that spouses feel threatened and resentful of these people and experiences and enthusiasms that have so captivated their husband or wife and have so excluded them.

A final hazard is that the long-established balance of power in the marriage may be upset by the trainee's increased sophistication. He or she may attempt to apply newly acquired knowledge or skills to intimidate or manipulate the partner. What used to be a fairly even give and take becomes a painful mismatch as the trainee interprets and labels and condescends and out-maneuvers their mate. One special case is when the trainee redefines the relationship as therapist-client. Even a mate who is in need of a therapist is likely to resent the loss of a spousal relationship in order to get one.

UTILIZING THERAPEUTIC SKILLS AS A NONTHREATENING RESOURCE FOR ONE'S OWN MARRIAGE

Every training program provides rich new perspectives and insights to participants that, wisely applied, might be of great benefit to the trainee's marital relationship. Presumably one is taught how to negotiate more mutual scripts, how to avoid or disengage from power struggles, how to check out one's perceptions of one's partner's feelings, and so forth. I have observed that trainees who follow the three following rules escape most of the potential damage discussed in the last section and may even profit maritally from their training.

(1) Trainee's marriages seem to thrive best when, no matter how demanding or engaging the training program is, they protect a regular time and some energy for the marriage. The actual amount of time seems to matter less than the regularity of it and the priority manifested by protecting it against all competing pressures. This signals to the spouse that the relationship remains a central value even in the face of all of the new ideas, experiences, and people who have suddenly become important to the trainee. Unambiguous, regular affirmation of that core commitment defuses jealousy, decreases defensiveness, and most importantly keeps the marital relationship itself alive and well. It has been truly said that the grass is always greenest where you water it.

(2) We have noted that frequently the comfortable, taken-for-granted values and lifestyles upon which one's marriage has been founded may be sharply challenged by the philosophy of the training program. The impact of this confrontation upon the marriage depends largely upon how the trainee handles it. Those who uncritically adopt the new "religion" and rush home to explain to their spouse how important it is that they too become converted encounter the greatest resistance and divisiveness. For their own as well as for their partner's sake it seems to be more effective to weigh each new idea against the old, integrating the parts that seem to make sense and reserving judgement or rejecting the parts that do not. To the greatest extent possible the spouse needs to be included in these deliberations (if willing).

Unfortunately there are programs that place the trainees under great pressure to accept their philosophy lock, stock, and barrel and interpret any reluctance to do so as resistance due to hangups. If the issues are important in the couple's system of values and the program is unyielding in its insistence, I strongly recommend dropping out and finding another program. In my opinion the field needs mature, critical thinkers, not groupies.

When spouses are willing to be recruited as consultants on how best to handle this sort of situation, the stress can bond the couple rather than divide them.

(3) The one set of therapeutic skills that can generally be applied directly to one's partner without fear of negative consequences is the skill to perceive what his or her wants and needs are and to administer a prolonged dose of positives to him or her based on this knowledge. It is hard to think of any other lesson that might not backfire if applied to one's mate. Practicing communication skills may be perceived as playing games or being phony. Attempts to negotiate behavioral exchange or new family rules may be seen as presumptuous or unsettling. Even new sexual technique or enthusiasms may arouse suspicion and resentment. But almost no one objects to having their needs met. In our experience this approach can go wrong only (a) if the trainee misreads the cues and incorrectly assesses the needs, or (b) if the trainee makes a big production of it so that he or she comes across as condescending or as the "suffering servant," or (c) if the trainee becomes overly concerned with the injustice and one-sidedness of it all. Actually, sooner or later the spouse is virtually certain to reciprocate spontaneously, but there is sometimes a lag between the investment and the payoff.

It should be clear, of course, that all spouses are not defensive and resistant against the ideas their trainee mates bring home. Some are excited from the beginning. In such cases a far more comprehensive and rewarding sharing can occur. Not uncommonly, such spouses are also recruited into the profession and become cotherapists or at least coprofessionals with their spouses.

SINGLE, DIVORCED, AND UNHAPPILY MARRIED TRIANGULAR THERAPISTS

It has been suggested by some, both within and without the field, that having a successful marriage of one's own is a major factor in one's probability of success as a marital therapist. They reason that only someone who has themselves mastered the calculus of success can teach others to master it. Further, they argue that only when anchored in the harbor of a secure and satisfying relationship can one reliably deal with all of the unsettling issues of transference and counter-transference. Finally, they point out that the issue of credibility with clients should make a difference in outcomes independent of any differential in skill of the therapist.

I am not aware of any research that has systematically tested this set of assumptions. My own observation is that personal qualities such as sensitivity, maturity, intelligence, self-confidence, and talent are what determines who are the great therapists and who the mediocre ones, who are the healers and who are the merely well-intended meddlers. Marital status per se does not, in my experience, predict competence.

It is not the life course itself but one's reaction to it that is the crucial variable. There are those who have never married but whose lives have been full and rich and whose human experience has provided them with compassion and sensitivity sufficient to compensate for their lack of concrete marital experience. I have, for example, known a number of members of Catholic religious orders, several homosexuals, and a number of other never-married people who were top-notch triangular therapists by any measure. Others in these same categories, of course, may have become embittered or disengaged or narrow in their world view in response to an apparently similar set of experiences.

For that matter, I have known happily married therapists who are not very good at what they do precisely because their life experiences have protected them from having to learn to deal with pain and frustration.

Among the divorced, I have known some who have been made wiser and more compassionate by the experience and others who have been so demoralized and defeated and have become so cynical or defensive as a result that they have been virtually ruined as therapists.

The case of those with ongoing chronic (or perhaps acute) marital difficulties is the hardest. Some are able to insulate their private life from their professional life very effectively (just as other professionals such as physicians and air traffic controllers and policemen and actors and teachers have to do). Indeed one might argue that the ability to segregate the compartments of their lives is central to the definition of a professional. Still, some find this too difficult. The very issues (fidelity, physical abuse, alcoholism, passive agressive neglect, etc.) that are their own daily crosses to bear are also the subject matter of the therapy sessions they conduct. The connections are too alive to be ignored and the pain from one's private life begins to intrude into the therapist's work with clients. Therapists finding themselves in this situation have an ethical responsibility to work on their own problems with a supervisor or therapist who can help sort out the various threads of their lives in a way that does not compromise their effectiveness as therapists.

The matter of credibility with the client may be an issue on occasion. Some clients are convinced that only someone who has been happily married for at least fifteen or twenty years can possibly know how to help them. They may open the first interview or even the initial phone contact with questions along these lines. In some cases the only thing for a therapist who doesn't meet their criteria to do is to refer them to a colleague who does. I recommend, however, that the client be invited to try three or four sessions and see whether, in fact, the therapist is able to be helpful.

a final word

It has been our premise that triangular therapy is different from other types of clinical practice. While therapies of every type must deal with the basic issues of rapport-building and intervention, when the client is a couple instead of a person issues are raised that simply don't come up in regular dyadic therapy. Questions of symmetry and therapist potency become central issues in the clinical process. Standard interventions need to be modified and adapted to meet the triangular reality. Even the therapist's own personal bonds may come to have a relevance that they would not in other therapeutic formats.

I feel strongly that the issues discussed in these pages are important ones for every triangular practitioner to consider. The recommendations offered, of course, do not exhaust the reservoir of possible effective solutions. Each therapist must choose a style that suits his or her own personality and talent. My hope is that novices in the field may have been stimulated to seek those solutions in their own idiom and that veteran colleagues will find interest in comparing their own experiences and conclusions with mine.

references

Bach, G. R., & Wyden, P. *The intimate enemy: How to fight fair in love and marriage.* New York: Avon, 1969.

Bockus, F. *Couple therapy.* New York: Jason Aronson, 1980.

Broderick, C. B. *Couples: How to confront problems and maintain loving relationships.* New York: Simon & Schuster, 1979. (a)

Broderick, C. B. *Marriage and the family.* Englewood Cliffs, N. J.: Prentice-Hall, 1979. (b)

Caplow, T. *Two Against one: Coalition in triads.* Englewood Cliffs, N.J.: Prentice Hall, 1968.

Ellis, A. *Growth through reason.* Palo Alto: CA: Science and Behavior Books, 1971.

Ellis, A. Techniques of handling anger in marriage. *Journal of Marriage and Family Counseling,* 1976, 2, 305-316.

Fagan, J. & Shepherd, I. L. (Eds.). *Gestalt therapy now: Theory, techniques, applications.* Palo Alto, CA: Science and Behavior Books, 1970.

Framo, J. L. The integration of marital therapy with sessions with family of origin. In A. S. Vuzman & D. P. Kniskern (Eds.) *Handbook of family therapy.* New York: Brunner/Mazel, 1981.

Freud, S. The future prospect of psychoanalytic therapy. In *Collected Papers,* Vol. II. New York: Basic Books, 1959. (Originally published, 1910.)

Freud, S. The dynamics of transference. In *Collected papers*, Vol. II. New York: Basic Books, 1959. (Originally published, 1915.)

Guerney, B. G. *Relationship enhancement.* San Francisco: Jossey-Bass, 1977.

Haley, J. Whither family therapy? *Family Process*, 1962, 1, 69-100.

Haley, J. *Uncommon therapy: The psychiatric techniques of Milton H. Ericson, M.D.* New York: Norton, 1973.

Heider, F. *The psychology of interpersonal relations.* New York: John Wiley, 1958.

Jacobson, N. S. & Margolin, G. *Marital therapy.* New York: Brunnel/Mazel, 1979.

Mace, D. Marital intimacy and the deadly love-anger cycle. *Journal of Marriage and Family Counseling*, 1976, 2, 131-138.

Miller, S., Nunnally, E. W., & Wackman, D. B. *Alive and aware: Improving communication in relationships.* Minneapolis: Interpersonal Communications Programs, 1975.

Minuchin, S. *Families and family therapy.* Cambridge, MA: Harvard University Press, 1974.

Newcomb, T. M. An approach to the study of communicative acts. *Psychological Review*, 1953, 60, 393-404.

O'Connor, P. A. *Coalition formation in conjoint marriage counseling.* Unpublished doctoral dissertation, University of Southern California, Department of Sociology, 1974.

Parsons, T. Family structure and the socialization of the child. In T. Parsons & R. Frederick Bales (Eds.) *Family, Socialization and Interaction Process.* New York: Free Press, 1955.

Pulliam-Krager, J. *Typification of clients by counselors.* Unpublished master's thesis, Department of Sociology, University of Southern California, 1974.

Rogers, C. R. *Client-centered therapy: Its current practice, implications and theory.* Boston: Houghton-Mifflin, 1951.

Satir, V. *People making.* Palo Alto, CA: Science and Behavior Books, 1972.

Straus, M. A. Leveling, civility and violence in the family. *Journal of Marriage and the Family*, 1974, 36, 13-29.

Stuart, R. B. Operant interpersonal program for couples. In D. H. Olson (Ed.) *treating Relationship.* Lake Mills, IA: Graphic Publishing, 1976.

Thomas, E. J. *Marital communication and decision-making: Analysis, assessment and change.* New York: Free Press, 1977.

Waller, W. *The family: A dynamic interpretation.* New York: Cordon, 1938.

Watzlawick, P., Beavin, J. H., & Jackson, D. D. *Pragmatics of human communication.* New York: Norton, 1967.

Watzlawick, P., Weakland, J., & Fisch, R. *Change: Principles of problem formation and problem resolution.* New York: Norton, 1974.

Wolff, K. H. (Ed.) *The Sociology of Georg Simmel.* New York: Free Press, 1950.

Zuk, G. *Family therapy: a triadic-based approach.* New York: Behavioral Books, 1971.

about the author

Carlfred B. Broderick graduated magna cum laude with a bachelor's degree in Social Relations from Harvard University in 1953, and obtained his Ph.D. in Child Development and Family Relations from Cornell in 1956. He also completed postdoctoral work in marriage counseling at the University of Minnesota during 1966-1967. He has held positions as Associate Professor of Family Development at the University of Georgia and Professor of Family Relationships at Pennsylvania State University. He is presently Professor of Sociology and Executive Director of the Ph.D. program in Marriage and Family Therapy at the University of Southern California in Los Angeles. Dr. Broderick has been editor of the *Journal of Marriage and the Family*, and President (1975-1976) of the National Council on Family Relations, and the Southern California Association of Marriage and Family Counselors. He is a Fellow of the American Association for Marriage and Family Therapy and the American Sociological Association.

In addition to over fifty research reports and theoretical presentations, his publications include six books: *The Individual, Sex, and Society,* edited with Jessie Bernard in 1969, *Sexuelle Entwickland in Kindheit und Jungend* (1970), *A Decade of Research and Action on the Family* (1971), *Couples: How to Confront Problems and Maintain Loving Relationships* (1979), and *Marriage and the Family* (1979 and 1983). He is listed in *Who's Who in America* and a number of other biographical books. Professor Broderick and Kathleen, his wife of 30 years, are the parents of eight children and have an increasing number of grandchildren.